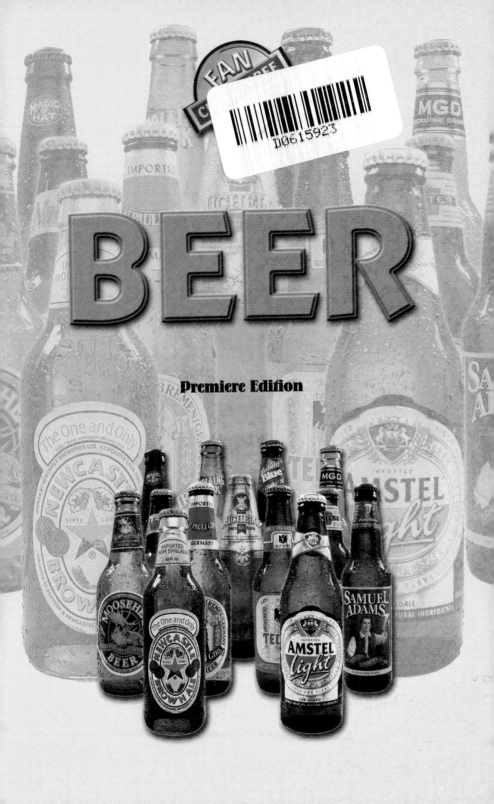

BEER

Premiere Edition

BEER

EDITORIAL

Managing Editor: Jeff Mahony
Associate Editors: Melissa A. Bennett
Jan Cronan
Gia C. Manalio
Mike Micciulla
Paula Stuckart
Assistant Editors: Heather N. Carreiro
Jennifer Renk
Joan C. Wheal
Editorial Assistants: Timothy R. Affleck
Beth Hackett
Christina M. Sette
Steven Shinkaruk

WEB
(CollectorsQuest.com)
Web Reporter: Samantha Bouffard
Web Graphic Designer: Ryan Falis

PRODUCTION
Production Manager: Scott Sierakowski

ART

Creative Director: Joe T. Nguyen
Assistant Art Director: Lance Doyle
Senior Graphic Designers: Marla B. Gladstone
Susannah C. Judd
David S. Maloney
Carole Mattia-Slater
David Ten Eyck
Graphic Designers: Jennifer J. Bennett
Sean-Ryan Dudley
Kimberly Eastman
Melani Gonzalez
Caryn Johnson
Jaime Josephiac
Jim MacLeod
Jeremy Maendel
Chery-Ann Poudrier

R&D

Product Development
Manager: Paul Rasid
R&D Specialist: Priscilla Berthiaume

ISBN 1-58598-066-8

CheckerBee
PUBLISHING

306 Industrial Park Road
Middletown, CT 06457

CollectorsQuest
•com

Table Of Contents

Introducing The CheckerBee Fan Guide™

Beer fans, like their preferred beverage, come in all shapes, sizes and styles. Are you a loyal "Bud man" or a self-styled "beer snob?" Are you just a casual drinker or do you brew your own double bocks in your basement? Do you collect vintage beer steins, cans, trays and other breweriana? Ever wonder how the big breweries make their magic?

The CheckerBee Fan Guide to Beer™ covers all this and much more. Inside you'll find profiles of the best brewers (microbrews and big guys too) in the United States, Mexico, Europe and Canada, including company histories and a look at their many brews. For your reading (and drinking) pleasure, the guide spotlights 50 great beers that are available in the United States, both domestics and imports.

Other great sections include a history of beer, a look at the brewing process from barley to bottle, and even a selection of great beer recipes. If you're a breweriana collector, you'll want to check out our spotlight of collectors and their beer memorabilia. This guide even provides secondary market values to give you an idea of how much your own collection might be worth or to inspire you to start collecting from scratch.

For the dedicated beer hunter, we've even included a special pull-out checklist of hundreds of different beers. You can keep track of the ones you've enjoyed and others that you might never have heard of.

You don't have to be a beer expert to find something in the CheckerBee Fan Guide™ to suit your taste. All you need is an appreciation for the world's greatest beverage!

Beer Through The Ages

When you look back through the hazy mists of time to the dawn of civilization through the Dark Ages, all the way to the modern day, beer has been with us every step of the way. This beverage's origins stretch all the way back to the ancient cultures of the Sumerians and Egyptians and continues to be a drink of choice throughout the world today.

An Ancient Brew

Somewhere around 10,000 B.C., humans decided to give up their hunter-gatherer lifestyle to settle down and become farmers. Evidence shows that barley was one of the first grains these farmers cultivated; but was it grown to make beer or bread? The debate rages on.

Stalks of grain look quite different than the beer they are made into.

Ancient Alcohol

Another popular ancient drink was mead. Mead, at its most basic level, is fermented honey and water.

Whichever came first, no one can doubt the importance of beer to ancient cultures – it was everywhere! Beer was a good source of nutrients and in many countries and civilizations, beer was considered a healthy alternative to water. Many water supplies were contaminated by contagious diseases, but once the water was boiled for the beer-making process, most of the bacteria were eliminated. Beer was also considered medicinal and was prescribed by many ancient societies. It also played a role in important religious and social ceremonies and was sometimes used as a form of payment. And you thought it was just for fun!

Archaeologists have discovered many ancient pictures and descriptions of early beer. Some pictures depict how beer was consumed through long, narrow straws to drink the beverage out of the bottom of a large bowl. The oldest

An early drinking vessel with straw.

Pyramid and the pyramids.

known written recipe for beer is written on a clay tablet and is part of an epic poem called *Hymn to Ninkasi*. The Babylonian Empire was also fond of beer, and the ancient Egyptians even buried beer in tombs for drinking during afterlife. Other ancient beer-drinking civilizations included the Native Americans (who made a corn-based beer), the Aztecs, Incans and Mayans, the Saxons, Vikings, Japanese, Chinese and Africans. Beer would remain the beverage of choice for thousands of years.

Hop On In

In medieval Britain, before the use of hops, all of the grain-based fermented beverages were called ale. These ales were flavored with all manner of spices, herbs and other plants, most of which were valued for medicinal properties. This mixture was called gruit and included things like honey, bog myrtle, nettles, yarrow and rosemary. Ale was the most popular beverage of the era and was consumed by everyone at all times of the day.

The earliest known written record of using hops in beer was in the mid 1100s in Germany by Abbess Hildegard von Bingen. Hops were not introduced to England until the early 1400s and were not widely accepted for many years. In fact, the British resisted the introduction of this new ingredient so much that it was outlawed due to a fear of its effects. It took some years before hops was again declared legal in England.

Brits And Their Beer

It's hard to imagine Britain without thinking of the local pub where people belly up to the bar for a good pint. Lager never quite caught on in England the way it did in the United States and Germany. Ale is king there,

Resurrecting Beer

According to the Associated Press, in 1990, Fritz Maytag, owner of Anchor Brewing Co., worked with archaeologists at the University of Pennsylvania to successfully recreate the Sumerian beer from the *Hymn to Ninkasi*. In 1996, the Egyptian Exploration Society, along with Scottish and Newcastle Breweries (makers of Newcastle Brown Ale), successfully reproduced ancient Egyptian beer.

or at least it was. CAMRA (Campaign for Real Ale) was formed in the early 1970s by a small group in England whose aim was to fight for consumers' rights, support the pub as a community center and promote the traditional beverage as a part of the country's culture and history. For the 50 years before CAMRA formed, no new ale breweries had opened in the United Kingdom and local pubs were disap-

pearing at an alarming rate. Since then, the organization has grown tremendously with foreign chapters in the United States, Canada, China, Belgium and Australia. Ale's future in Britain is now much brighter.

In a tavern, the bartender is the picture of hospitality.

One ale style that developed in England is porter. The story goes that Ralph Harwood, a London brewer and pub landlord in the early 1700s, invented the style by combining the results of three mashings. It is believed that at this time in England the same mash was used three times with each rinse, lessening the potency of the beverage – the first product, "ale," was the strongest, then "beer," then "two penny," the weakest. Because the three mashings were combined, the result was often called "entire" beer.

The name of porter came from its popularity with the workers who toted wares in the produce market, called "porters." Porter eventually decreased in popularity but today has been revived by home and craft brewers.

Bavarian Beer

Germany has a long history of beer making and beer drinking. The Germans invented lager and many of the popular beer styles we drink today. The German Purity Law, or Reinheitsgebot, of 1516 is well known and respected throughout the world.

Taverns Of Olde

The origin of the tavern lies with the Romans. When they invaded Britain, they not only built roads but established these taverns that served as inns for weary travelers to sleep and imbibe. Taverns eventually became community centers.

It was passed by Duke Wilhelm IV of Bavaria and is the oldest food law in the world. It proclaims that the only ingredients to be used in beer are barley, hops and water.

Oktoberfest is a celebration that is enjoyed by people all over the world.

The Germans are also famous for Oktoberfest – the largest public festival in the world. This event is held annually and draws visitors from around the world. It all began with the marriage of Crown Prince Ludwig of Bavaria (later King Ludwig I) to Princess Therese of Saxony-Hildburghausen on October 12, 1810. The celebration was held in Munich on the fields in front of the city gates. The big event was a series of horse races that concluded the festivities. Today, horse races are no longer part of the celebration, but the festivities continue nonetheless with plenty of beer, food and fun.

Women & Beer

According to a 1995 study by *Brewing Techniques* magazine, there were only 10 women brewers from nine different brewpubs in the United States. This may not surprise anyone – after all, beer is for men, isn't it? Well . . . no. In fact, in early cultures, people didn't see things that way at all. Women were the original brewers of beer. Many cultures even attribute the invention of beer to women – and goddesses. It was during the Middle Ages, when monasteries began to adopt the brewing process that men became more involved with beer. By the early 1600s, the trade had pretty much fully shifted to a male-run business.

Dust Off Your Lederhosen!

The year 2001 will mark the 168th Oktoberfest and will span from the 22nd of September to the 7th of October. In 1999, there were 6.5 million visitors who drank over 6 million liters of beer and consumed over 600,000 units of chicken and about 150,000 pairs of sausages!

It is said that the *Mayflower* landed at Plymouth Rock in search of beer.

Beer Conquers The New World

While it's probably not the story you heard in history class, it is believed by some that the reason the Pilgrims landed the Mayflower in 1620 at Plymouth, instead of their original destination farther south, because they were running out of important supplies, including beer. This has even been documented! The beer the colonists made was dependent on whatever ingredients were available, including oats, corn, pumpkins and molasses. From this point on, most beer was made at home, by women, until commercial breweries took over. New Amsterdam, now New York City, had its own breweries already by the early 1600s.

Lager was first introduced to the United States in the 1840s from Germany. The style had originated in Germany much earlier, when monks began storing beer in caves through the summer. This style has dominated the U.S. beer market ever since.

Saintly Brew

Several saints have been connected with beer. Saint Brigid reputedly turned bath water into ale for a colony of lepers through prayer. Hildegard von Bingen, who first wrote about hops, was also sainted.

Yet the booming beers business met some obstacles. The 18th Amendment, known as Prohibition, changed the face of U.S. brewing for decades to come. This 13-year period, from 1920 to 1933, was devastating to the brewing industry. Some breweries survived by branching out into soda or other products, some brewed illegal beer, but most closed their doors, never to reopen. After World War II, regional brands began to decline even further

Many famous men supported both the U.S. Constitution and beer brewing.

as they either closed or were bought out by larger national companies.

Yet in the 1980s times began to change and the "Beer Renaissance" began. In recent years, brewpubs, craft breweries and micro-breweries have been sprouting up all over the country and are reviving many old and extinct beer styles.

Important Discoveries

> ### Beer And Weddings
>
> The word "bridal" comes from the practice of beer being brewed for a wedding ("bride ale") and being sold by the bride's family. The proceeds of this sale went to the newlyweds.

Many important scientific discoveries and inventions have made beer the way it is today. Did you know that Louis Pasteur originally conducted his studies to aid beer making? His studies played a huge part in the learning about the fermentation process. In 1876, Pasteur published the results of his study. In 1888, Emile Hansen, a Danish botanist, published an article detailing how he grew a pure yeast culture. The yeast strain that he isolated was later used to make lagers.

> ### Patriot Brewers
>
> Many colonial patriots and statesmen were interested in brewing, including George Washington (whose recipe for beer can be seen at the New York Public Library), Samuel Adams, Thomas Jefferson and William Penn, the founder of Pennsylvania who started its first brewery.

Beer has been put into bottles, either made of glass or stone, since at least the mid-1500s. The earliest mention comes from an unconfirmed tale of Alexander Nowell, the Dean of St. Paul's Cathedral in London, who misplaced a bottle while fishing. When Nowell later found it he realized that the carbonation had increased and the beer had remained fresh. Just how did he realize that the carbonation had increased? Well, when he opened the bottle, it made quite a sound! In fact it was so loud that it has been referred to as the sound of a gun!

Old stone beer bottles.

The development of refrigeration enabled

the manufacture of refrigerated trucks and railroad cars. Now beer could be distributed nationally.

A modern-day crown cap.

The crown cap, which allowed easier sealing of bottles and helped preserve the beer, was patented in 1892 by William Painter. This was the first step toward promoting home consumption. This trend continued as the first aluminum can was introduced in 1935 by the Kreuger Brewing Co. of New Jersey.

Perhaps the biggest step in beer promotion was the introduction of national television and radio advertising. This provided national-brand recognition and was perhaps the beginning of the end for local breweries. The all-important pull tab wasn't invented until 1962 and was introduced by the Pittsburgh Brewing Company. To reach even further into the market, other beer types have been developed for drinkers, such as light beers (for the calorie-conscious crowd) and dry beer.

Examples of light and dry beers.

Seasonal Lagers

Before the advent of refrigeration, beer was seasonal. It was made in the cooler months, usually September through March or April, and stored through the warmer months. Many beer names reflect this practice including the French Bière de Mars and the German Märzen or Oktoberfest beers.

As you have seen, the history of beer has taken on a life of its own. Read on to learn more about the people that are making the beer and those who are drinking it today.

Brewers Big And Small

From the end of Prohibition in 1933 through to the 1970s, the brewing landscape was dominated by megabreweries – Anheuser-Busch, Coors and Miller. However, beginning in the late 1970s, microbreweries and brewpubs began springing up on the West Coast and eventually made their way across the country. The 1980s and the 1990s saw brewpub numbers continue to

There's a lot that goes on inside a brewery.

increase. Yet, whether it takes place in a megabrewery or a microbrewery, the brewing process is pretty much the same. So what distinguishes the two from each other?

Barrels Of Beer On The Wall

In the world of brewing, size does matter! Most everything at a megabrewery is large, from the size of the brewing equipment to the brewery's square footage to the number of employees. One of the biggest differences between a megabrewery and a microbrewery is the brewery's annual volume. This amount is expressed in barrels (one barrel is the approximate equivalent of 31 gallons). It's gener-

ally accepted that a microbrewery produces less than 15,000 barrels annually, a regional brewery produces from 15,000 to 500,000 barrels annually and a megabrewery produces 500,000 or more barrels each year.

Literally, hundreds of barrels of beer on the wall.

In terms of production, Budweiser towers over the competition.

Sometimes the lines between the different types of breweries aren't very clear, especially in the eyes of the beer-drinking public. Most people are less concerned with numbers and statistics and more interested in the end results. People tend to think of regional breweries as microbreweries, since they also are often in the business of making craft or specialty beers. Because of the rapid growth in the microbrewing industry, the guidelines defining breweries have been revised several times, increasing the maximum number of barrels that a microbrewery or regional brewery can produce. The numbers are also deceptive when you take into account the large gap between the smallest and the largest megabrewers. The world's largest brewery, Anheuser-Busch, produces more than 80 million barrels annually compared to the 500,000 barrels or so that might be produced in one year by the smallest megabrewery.

Keep On Truckin'

Of course, there is a reason why Anheuser-Busch and its megabrewery buddies brew so much beer – beer is popular and they know they can sell it! Megabrews are more widely available and have larger distribution channels than smaller breweries' products do, and megabreweries can even stretch their distribution into the international market. It is relatively easy to go into any liquor store in the United States and purchase Budweiser, but depending on where you live, beers like Magic Hat #9 or Saranac Pale Ale may be harder to find. In some cases, microbrewers look to megabrewers for help in expanding their distribution area.

Many megabrewers facilitate their wide distribution by having several brewing plants located in different areas of the country and even in other countries. They can also own part or all of a transportation company, a packaging com-

Anheuser-Busch distributes both Bud and Red Hook.

pany and a bottle or can manufacturing company, giving them direct control over distribution every step of the way. For the beer fan, this mass production means lower prices at the package store or supermarket, especially in comparison with many microbrewery beers.

Bigger Doesn't Always Mean Better

But the generally higher prices of microbrews hasn't hurt their popularity any. The appeal of the microbrew is its distinctiveness. While megabrews are mass produced with consistent results in order to appeal to the largest number of consumers, microbrews tend to focus on hand-crafted specialty beer. They tend to use fewer or no adjuncts (like corn or rice), additives or preservatives, make smaller batches of their beer and promote

There are many microbreweries that brew many types of beer.

themselves as having a more "hands-on" brewing process. Many of the smaller microbreweries do not pasteurize their beer, which results in a more flavorful beer that appeals to many drinkers.

Microbrewers are eager and willing to experiment with different ingredients and beer styles. The microbrewery movement has rekindled an appreciation for many traditional beer styles and is responsible for introducing many European styles to the American public that few had ever experienced before. In fact, these "new" styles have become so popular that many megabreweries have created new product lines in an effort to compete with microbreweries! They have done this either by producing the beer themselves or by buying up small microbreweries.

Brewmasters take their job very seriously.

Of course, money is less of an object to megabreweries, who tend to have larger budgets for

The New Belgium Brewing Company sponsors local events to publicize the brewery.

national advertising campaigns, usually on television. Few microbreweries can compete with this sort of advertising. If they do advertise, it is usually at the local or regional level, and probably in print or over the radio. Microbreweries rely largely on the Internet, word of mouth and their local image. Often microbreweries will capitalize on their role as a part of the local flavor and will sponsor concerts, marathons or the like. This way they get their name in print, and are associated with something that is seen as positive for the community.

Other Beer Businesses

Brewpubs are another form of beer business that also saw a revival beginning in the 1970s. Brewpubs consist of a restaurant and a brewing facility all at one location. Patrons can enjoy freshly brewed beer, usually pulled by a draft system straight from the tanks, with their meals. Many brewpubs offer tours of their brewing facilities and often the equipment can be seen from the eating area. Some brewpubs are able to sell their beer for off-premise consumption, depending on local and state laws (but if these sales exceed 50 percent of their total production, the brewpub is then considered to be a microbrewery).

Some popular breweries started out as brewpubs. The Deschutes Brewery originally opened its doors as a Bend, Oregon, brewpub in 1988. Thanks to positive word of mouth from patrons, demand for the pub's brews increased dramatically. Deschutes brewed 310 barrels in its inaugural year. Just 10 years later, that number was close to 80,000 barrels. Other times, an established brewery chooses to open a brewpub.

Deschutes Brewery, maker of Black Butte Porter, was a brewpub that grew to become a full-fledged brewery.

For example, the Jacob Leinenkugel Brewing Company, which has been brewing beer since the 1800s, waited until 1998 to set up a brewpub. Located next to Bank One Ballpark in Phoenix, Leinenkugel's Ballyard Brewery has become a popular postgame attraction for fans of the Arizona Diamondbacks baseball team.

Another type of brewer is the contract brewer. A good example of this is the Boston Beer Company, brewer of Samuel Adams. The Samuel Adams label goes on the beer, the Boston Beer Company dictates the recipe and ingredients and handles all of the marketing, sales and distribution, but several different breweries around the country make the beer for them. Confusingly enough, the term "contract brewer" has been used to describe both the company who offers the contract and the breweries who are contracted by them. Most contract brewers are microbreweries or regional breweries.

The Jacob Leinenkugel Brewing Co. combined beer with baseball.

As long as Americans continue to develop their taste for hand-crafted brews, the growth of smaller breweries and brewpubs will continue. Meanwhile, megabreweries are producing more craft-type beers to cater to the changing palates of the American public. Whatever you might think of microbrews or megabrews, the end result is tastier beer and better selection for beer fans everywhere!

The Boston Beer Company, which brews Samuel Adams, is a contract brewer.

Tour A Brewpub!

The Elm City Brewing Company in Keene, New Hampshire, is a brewpub that counts among its brews Millcreek Wheat, Raspberry Wheat, Lunch Pail Ale, Irish Stout, Oktoberfest Lager, Brickyard ESB and Texas Brown. It's called a

The outside of the Elm City Brewing Company.

brewpub because it's a business that not only brews beer but also has a restaurant (and a gift shop, too).

Elm City Brewing has a dining room and a "beer hall," from which patrons can watch virtually all of the brewing process.

Some of the action happens behind the scenes, however, such as the fermentation and condition process, in which the beer needs to remain undisturbed for a period of time. When the beer is ready for consumption, it is drained directly into giant serving tanks, which are huge, industrial-sized containers manufactured specifically for the brewing process. The serving tanks are connected to the taps at the bar from which your beer is served.

The beer in these serving tanks is what gets poured into your glass.

Those beer steins over the bar belong to members of the Mug Club.

At the Elm City Brewing Company, the activities aren't just limited to watching beer get made, eating and drinking, though. Patrons can also become members of a Mug Club, which entitles members to special privileges, such as larger servings of beer than regular customers get!

Non-Alcoholic Brews, Hard Lemonades And Hard Ciders

It Looks Like Beer, It Smells Like Beer . . .

For some people, they're the liquid equivalent of unsalted rice cakes. For others, they're a crisp, refreshing, judgment-friendly alternative to beer or even soda. Of course, we're talking about non-alcoholic brews, the malted beverages that taste like beer but have a much smaller alcohol content.

Here is a sample of non-alcoholic brews.

Stroll down the beer aisle of your local supermarket and you'll see a wide variety of non-alcoholic brews. The largest domestic breweries offer non-alcoholic brews, such as Busch Non-Alcoholic, Coors Non-Alcoholic, O'Doul's and O'Doul's Amber (Anheuser-Busch) and Sharp's (Miller). And there are also some notable imports which make non-alcoholic brews, including Buckler (Heineken Brewery), Clausthaler (Binding Brewery), Haake-Beck (Beck's Brewing Co.), Kaliber (Guinness), Molson Excel and St. Pauli Non-Alcoholic.

Take a good look at a non-alcoholic brew bottle and you'll notice that the word "beer" never appears on the label. That's because federal regulations restrict the alcohol content of non-alcoholic brews to less than 0.5% and prohibit them from being called "beer." Instead, drinks like O'Doul's and Sharp's are called "brews" or "malted beverages." Non-alcoholic brews, then, do contain a small amount of alcohol, but no more than many fruit juices and ciders (yes, there is alcohol in these products, believe it or not!).

O'Doul's is a non-alcoholic brew.

The most common method of crafting these malt beverages is to brew them just like beer, then remove the alcohol by boiling processes or through centrifugal heating systems. Another method is through arrested fermentation, in which yeast activity (which forms the alcohol content) is literally frozen early in the fermentation process.

The big knock on non-alcoholic brews is that they don't really taste like beer. There's some truth to this, due to the limitations of the brewing process, but the best non-alcoholic brews come very close to the real thing. Just like their beery brothers, these brews vary in flavor, body and bitterness – providing a little something for everyone, and with much less alcohol.

Not Your Grandma's Lemonade

But man (and woman) cannot live on beer alone. If you're in the mood for something sweet, there are a many different brands of hard lemonade to choose from. This beverage has recently won a place on package store and supermarket shelves, and has become immensely popular with everyone from 20-somethings to more mature drinkers.

A Doc Otis billboard advertisement towers over a building.

The idea of combining alcohol and citrus juice is not new, but only recently have brewers tried to sell ready-made hard lemonade directly to consumers. Since its debut in 1992, Coors Brewing Co.'s Zima had been the most popular alcoholic citrus beverage around.

Mike's Hard Lemonade was at the forefront of the lemonade craze.

But it was the appearance of Mike's Hard Lemonade in early 2000 that knocked Zima from its perch and triggered an explosion of hard lemonade pioneers that included both large and small operations alike. Among the brands available are Doc Otis' Hard Lemon, Henry's Hard Lemonade, Hooper's Hootch Lemon Brew, Jed's Hard Pink Lemonade, Rick's Spiked Lemonade and Two Dogs Lemonade Brew.

Most of these beverages range from 5 to 5.5% alcohol by volume, slightly higher than most beers. If pure lemon doesn't tickle your taste buds, you can choose from other hard fruit beverages, such as Two Dogs Orange Brew.

Apple Juice With a Kick

Hard cider has been around for a long time (almost as long as apples themselves!) and was an American favorite from the earliest colonial days. After a decline in popularity (lasting almost 100 years), hard cider has recently enjoyed a resurgence as people increasingly look for new flavors to satisfy their taste buds.

Cider Jack also comes in six pack form.

A delicious drink made from fermented apples, hard cider can vary greatly in body and tartness. Most commercial brands are between 4 and 6% alcohol by volume and are typically lightly carbonated. Some brands have additives or are made with apple concentrate, while others are more "pure."

With the recent popularity of hard cider in the United States, several brewers and wine makers have jumped head first into the cider ring, including the Boston Beer Company. However, most ciders are produced by specialized cider companies, a fair number of which are based in the apple-laden northern United States.

Among the more common domestic and imported brands available are Ace Apple Cider, Cider Jack Hard Cider, George Hornsby's Pubdraft's Draft Cider, HardCore Cider, Woodchuck Draft Cider and Woodpecker English Cider. Some of these come in different flavors and textures, such as Cider Jack Raspberry Hard Cider, HardCore Cranberry Cider and Woodchuck Draft Cider – Granny Smith.

A poster advertises Woodchuck Draft Cider.

The Brewing Process

Beer making is one of the oldest professions, dating back at least 7,000 years. In all that time, the process and ingredients haven't changed very much. However you look at it, brewing beer comes down to feeding treated grain (usually barley) to hungry yeast cells, who then produce carbon dioxide and, most importantly, alcohol!

While brewers may tweak the brewing process depending on the kind of beer they're trying to produce, the process is pretty standard throughout the industry. At its simplest level, brewing uses four basic ingredients: barley, water, hops and yeast.

Magic Hat uses giant tanks to make its beer.

Step One: Malting

Brewers and professional maltsters (who sell their malted barley to brewers) usually begin by loading the barley into a sealed tank where the barley is soaked in water. Traditionally, it was then laid out on the "growing floor," turned by hand and allowed to germinate, or to grow shoots. Today, however, modern breweries use sealed boxes that automatically turn the grain.

The grain is then heated to stop the germination process, and *voilà* – you now have malted barley (or "malt")! Brewers may let the

The barley begins its journey to become beer here.

now-dried malt roast for a bit in a kiln, to add flavor to the malt before it is milled or cracked. The milling process opens the barley kernels and results in a product known as grist. The grist is then transferred to a large vessel called a mash tun or mash mixer.

Transferring from tank to tank at the Elm City Brewing Co. facility.

Step Two: Mashing

Hot water is then pumped into the mash tun in order to stimulate the reaction that converts the starchy barley kernels into fermentable sugar. At this point, the brewer may add other grains or malts, such as wheat or rye, to add different colors and flavors to the beer. Some grains, like corn grits, have to be boiled in a cereal cooker before being added to the mash tun.

The mashing tun is a critical stage of the brewing process.

The now-thickened mixture of grains and water, called mash, has to pass a big survival test in the mash tun. Brewers must carefully regulate the temperature of the mixture or else risk destroying the entire tank of fledgling beer!

Once the mashing process is complete, the mixture is filtered to separate the husks and spent grain from the sweet liquid called "wort." Small breweries usually filter the wort right through the bottom of the mash tun. Most large breweries use a separate filtering vessel called the lauter tun. Then the wort is pumped into the brewery's main attraction – the brew kettle.

Step Three: Boiling

The brew kettle, or copper, is usually the largest tank in the brewery and is the place where the wort is boiled. Two very important steps happen at the boiling stage. First, hops are added to counteract

the wort's sweetness and add the bitter flavor and hoppy aroma that beer lovers expect from their favorite brew. The addition of hops is very much an art form. Not only do different types of hops lend different colors, flavors and aromas, but the hops will affect the brew differently depending on when they're added in the boiling process.

The brew kettle is where hops are added to the beer.

The second important part of the boiling stage is sterilization, as contamination could have occurred at any previous point in the brewing process. After one to two hours of boiling, the mixture is filtered again to separate the hops and other matter from the wort. This is done either through a trap-door filter or, more commonly, in a centrifuge called a whirlpool. The whirlpool separates out the sediment by spinning the wort rapidly. Following separation, the wort is sent to a wort chiller or heat exchanger where it is rapidly cooled down. Next, the cooled wort (sometimes called bitter wort because of the hops) is pumped into a large fermenter or fermentation tank, where it nears the end of its long road to beer-dom!

After the boiling stage, the wort is ready for fermentation.

Step Four: Fermentation

In the fermenter, live yeast is pitched (added) to the wort mixture. The yeast goes to work, consuming the sugar in the wort and releasing carbon dioxide and alcohol as by-products.

The Magic Hat Brewery (pictured) uses open-air fermentation.

Several factors and techniques affect the bubbling brew at this stage. Most commercial brewers use oversized, sealed tanks to ferment the wort, allowing only a release valve to relieve the pressure of the churning carbon dioxide. Other brewers (primarily European) use an open-air technique, called spontaneous fermentation, in which the wort ferments uncovered and airborne yeast can settle into the mix. This technique is especially popular among brewers of Belgian ales.

Another important factor is the type of yeast used for fermentation. Top-fermenting yeast rises to the top of the liquid after fermentation and produces ales, while bottom-fermenting yeast settles on the bottom of the tank and produces lagers. Temperature again plays a factor, as top-fermenting yeast is most well-suited to warmer temperatures, while bottom-fermenting yeast is best in cooler temperatures.

A glimpse of the fermentation tanks at Elm City Brewing Co.

The primary fermentation process takes anywhere from two to ten days depending on the style of beer desired. When this time constraint is met, the beer is filtered once again – this time to remove some of the yeast and other sediments. Then the beer is transferred to a conditioning or aging tank to mature.

Step Five: Conditioning

Depending on the kind of beer brewed, conditioning could last from as little as a few weeks to as much as a few months. Again, temperature is very important and must be continuously monitored. The conditioning or aging stage gives the beer time to develop complex flavors and aromas, as well as additional carbonation.

The Magic Hat Brewery boasts a large bottling area.

Once the beer is fully matured, it is filtered once again to remove the yeast that has settled in the aging tank. Now it's time to package up the beer. Most large breweries pasteurize the beer either before or after it is bottled or canned (kegged beer as well as microbrews typically aren't pasteurized). The process involves heating the beer to over 100°F in order to stop the yeast from continuing their fermentation and to kill bacteria and other contaminants that could be harmful. This is done either with prolonged heating at a lower temperature, or with an intense burst of heat sustained for a shorter time. This intense, short process is called flash pasteurization. The benefit of pasteurization is that it provides a longer shelf-life for the beer. The downside is that the excessive heat also kills some of the flavor.

Ah...finally the beer is ready to be tasted!

Once the beer is filtered and pasteurized, it's ready to be pumped into kegs, bottles or cans, and consumed by thirsty brewery tourists and consumers alike all over the country!

Home Brewing Tips For Fun And, Well . . . Fun!

L ucky for us, home brewing became legal in the United States in 1979. However, there are about 30 states whose laws may supersede the federal ones, so it's sometimes hard to tell whether home-brewing is a legal activity or not. It's best to check with your local and state governments as to the legalities of home brewing before you begin or are arrested!

Home-brewing is exciting and fun!

Getting Started

Brewing beer at home is an exciting process, as it gives a great sense of accomplishment and produces high-quality beer. The brewing process is always the same, no matter what level of brewing you are at, or what type of beer you are brewing. The variations in the types and flavors of beer come from differing ingredients. Even as a beginner, if you follow the strict guidelines of brewing, you'll be able to create a great-tasting beer.

Some of the supplies you need to home-brew.

The first step in starting home-brewing is to invest in a home-brewing kit, which can be purchased at a home-brewing supply shop or through the Internet or mail order. A good home-brewing kit can be purchased for under $100, (although they are available in a large price range).

WHAT YOU NEED:

Big cooking pot (at least 3 gallons) with cover, or brew pot

Medium-sized pot

Wooden spoon

Small bowl or other container with air-tight cover

Fermentation bucket

Bottles and bottle caps

The next step after getting your home-brewing kit is to gather all the ingredients for your first batch of beer. Like the brewing kit, ingredients can be purchased either at a home-brewing supply shop or via the Internet or mail order. The ingredients can likely be purchased in a kit to make things easier for you. Kits are sold by type of beer, and for your first time it is generally recommended that you brew an ale, as they are pretty easy to brew.

Here are some of the ingredients necessary for home-brewing.

INGREDIENTS:

2 3.3-lb. cans of hopped liquid malt extract (which should come with its own package of yeast)

Several gallons of bottled water (you can use tap water, but the minerals and additives sometimes found in tap water can alter the flavor of your beer)

Cleanliness Is Next To Godliness

Once you have the equipment and ingredients all set, the next step is to clean all of your equipment thoroughly. Sterilize and sanitize everything. Bacteria is harmful to brewing as it ruins the quality and texture of beer. The area that you're brewing in should also be as bacteria-free as possible. Remember – anything that comes in contact with beer should be clean, so wash your hands frequently during the brewing process.

(If you want to brew beer but are not ready to make the commitment of purchasing a kit, you may want to see if there is a "brew on premises" outfit near you, which allows you to go and use the facility's equipment, recipes and ingredients.)

Ready, Set, Brew!

Home-brewing is not a long process, but patience is still necessary. Don't hurry things along, no matter how eager you are. That said, here's how to brew your first batch of beer.

• Fill your big cooking pot or brew pot with 2.5 gallons of the bottled water, place it on the largest burner of your stove and bring it to a boil.

• In the meantime, heat the hopped liquid malt extract. The best way is to place the cans in a medium-sized cooking pot filled with warm water (you can use tap water for this step). Heating the hopped liquid malt extract will soften it up and make it easier to pour.

Making the wort.

• When the water in the big cooking pot comes to a boil, add in the hopped liquid malt extract and stir vigorously.

If your recipe calls for it, filter your wort with a cheesecloth.

• Bring this mixture to a boil and leave it uncovered for one hour, stirring occasionally.

• After one hour, take the pot off the burner and place the cover on it. Congratulations! You have now created an important beer ingredient, wort.

• But it's not over yet! The wort needs to cool – and quickly! Cooling as quickly as possible is necessary to inhibit bacteria growth. The best way to do this is to fill your sink with cold water and immerse the covered pot in it. Keep checking the temperature of the water in the sink. When it feels warm, drain it and add cold water.

• While you're doing this, open up the packet of yeast and dump it in a cup of lukewarm (approximately 80° F) bottled water. Stir gently and let it stand for 10 minutes in an airtight container. This process is known as "proofing" and prepares the yeast for fermentation.

Adding the yeast.

• When your wort has been sufficiently cooled, pour it into the fermentation bucket (make sure the spigot is in a closed position). Add enough cold bottled water so that the wort rises to about the 4.5-gallon mark. Check that the temperature of the mixture is about 70° F. Add another half gallon of bottled water to the fermentation bucket, altering the temperature if necessary, so that there are five gallons of wort at about 70° F.

• Pour the yeast into the cooled wort, being sure to distribute it in a wide circle to disperse it well. You have now started the fermentation process!

• Cover the fermentation bucket with its lid, and put it in a cool, dark place where it won't be disturbed. Your basement or an infrequently used closet are some really good options.

Patience Is A Virtue

Now you have to wait for seven days. On the seventh day, look for bubbles in the fermentation bucket. If a minute or so elapses between the bubbles, you can plan to bottle the next day! If after seven days, the float piece on the fermentation bucket is not floating, guess what? You can start bottling that day!

The tools you need to bottle your beer.

Once you have gotten the hang of the brewing process, read up about the intricacies of the brewing process and different beers. Remember, the process doesn't vary much, only the ingredients do. But don't worry – you'll be an expert brewer in no time!

Become A Beer Connoisseur

There is something very satisfying about cracking open an icy cold beer and guzzling it down. It doesn't take much to figure out whether or not you like the taste of that beer. But do you know that there are all sorts of factors that influence the way a beer tastes? Of course, your taste buds have a great deal to do with it, but there are several other factors that influence the flavor. For example, the beer's ingredients and the fermentation and aging process play a vital part in the taste. And then there are the less obvious factors. First of all, the beer's style, which is determined by color and degree of bitterness, is key. Also, the way the beer is stored and the temperature at which it is served both play a big part. And to top it off, the glass into which the beer is poured can affect its flavor.

We are going to start out with a look at the two most popular styles of beer – ales and lagers. We will then move on to see just how these other factors come into play in helping you make the decision of what tastes good.

Good For What "Ales" You

If you are craving a beer that is fruity and robust with a complex flavor and aroma, than an ale may be just what you are looking for. To establish this flavor, ales are produced with a top-fermenting yeast

Newcastle Brown Ale is a brown ale.

and are aged for a shorter period of time and at a warmer temperature than lagers. Within the family of ales, there are several types. Some are easily recognizable with the word "ale" as part of their name, while others are not so terribly obvious.

Ales are often named by color and are categorized by taste. **Brown ales** range from copper to brown in color and have a medium body and low hop bitterness. The less-common southern English version, is a darker and sweeter beer with a lighter body. American brown ales have a higher hop bitterness and aroma. **Pale ales** like Saranac Pale Ale, on the other hand, range in color from light golden to copper and have low-to-medium maltiness and high hop bitterness. Pale ale comes in different varieties: English, American and Indian.

There are also **porters**, such as Yuengling Porter, which are medium-bodied beers with a strong roasted-malt flavor. Porters range from brown to black and from dry to sweet. **Stouts** (Guinness is a familiar example) are derivatives of porters. Stouts are made with roasted unmalted barley and are slightly darker and fuller-bodied. They are available in dry, sweet and imperial varieties. There are also **wheat beers**, such as Widmer Brothers Hefeweizen, which are made with wheat rather than barley. Wheat beers are golden or amber in color with an effervescent consistency.

Waiting Longer For The Lager

If you are looking for a smoother, mellower flavor with more carbonation, then the lagers are for you. Most of the popular domestic brands are lagers (a German word meaning "storehouse"). This beer is brewed with a bottom-fermenting yeast and is aged for a longer period of time and at a cooler temperature than an ale.

Whereas ales are often categorized by their color, lagers boast of their nationality. You are probably very familiar with **American lagers** , such as Budweiser and Coors. These beers are highly carbonated and come in two varieties: pale and dark. The pale lagers are lighter in color, light-bodied with low levels of hop and malt

American and German lagers.

aroma and flavor. The dark lagers, on the other hand, are copper to brown in color, light to medium-bodied and have slightly more hop and malt flavor. There are also **German lagers**, such as Beck's, which are available in either pale or dark versions, as well. The pale versions range in color from straw to golden, in bitterness from low to medium and are medium-bodied. The dark versions range from copper to brown in color and have a moderate hop bitterness.

There are many more styles to be explored, including hybrids, such as Fat Tire Amber Ale, and specialty brews, such as fruit, herb, spice and smoked beer. In addition, there are also several sub-styles within the familiar ale and lager categories. These will tempt your taste buds, as well as increase your knowledge of the world of beer – so experiment and have some fun!

Keeping It Fresh

Now that you know a bit about the beer and what you like, you need to know what to do to preserve its flavor. Storing the beer properly is the first step. Remember that drastic temperature changes and overexposure to light can affect the beer's quality. Keep your "brewskies" in a cool, dark place – the refrigerator is best. Bottling or expiration dates are now printed on many bottles and cans (you may be familiar with the Budweiser "born on" date). So check the date on your beer – just like your bottle of milk!

Some signs of stale beer are obvious. "Skunky" or "skunked" beer is noticeable by its rancid smell, which is caused by exposure to ultraviolet light and most often afflicts beer in clear or light-colored glass bottles. Other unpleasant aromas such as that of damp cardboard or paper result from overexposure to oxygen. Appearance of floating flakes or cloudy material may be an indication that your beer is past its prime (although some beers are brewed to appear this way). Another warning sign is poor head formation and retention. Keep in mind that some beers do not form large heads and if this occurs, it may be the result of detergent residue or dirt on the glass.

The Presentation

The glass can also affect your drinking enjoyment. Using a glass moderates the amount of carbonation in the beer, making it easier to appreciate its aroma and to admire its color and clarity. It is important that your glass is large enough to fit the beer and its resulting

head. It isn't recommended that you use an ice-frosted glass as this will water down your beer and make it so cold you won't be able to taste it.

Temperature is also important. If your beer is too cold, its flavor and aroma will be dulled. As a general rule of thumb, ales should be chilled between 44°F and 52°F and lager between 42°F and 48°F. Pouring beer can also be tricky. Some beers are highly carbonated, sport large heads or both and should be poured slowly down the side of a tilted glass – unless you want a miniature foam volcano! Now that you've got it in your glass, it's time to put it to a taste test.

The Results

Take a look at the color and clarity of the beer by holding it up to the light, keeping in mind that some beers are meant to be cloudy. Also observe the size and longevity of the head. Check to see if it conforms to its style.

Now it's the moment you've been waiting for – take a sip. Make sure the beer reaches all areas of the tongue since sweet, bitter, salty and sour are tasted on different locations. Check if the sweetness of the malt and bitterness of the hops is balanced. Also note the after-taste, or the "finish."

You may want to take a separate sip to analyze the "mouthfeel" and "body" of the beer. The body may be light and fizzy (light-bodied) or robust and chewy (full-bodied). Most beers fall somewhere in between and are called medium-bodied. Once again, it all comes down to style.

The last step is rendering your final judgement. This is all you – no matter how you do it, the most important thing is to enjoy yourself!

About The Beers

O n the following pages, we feature 50 popular beer brands in the United States, both domestic and imported. This list is based on recent market-share data and the opinions of beer retailers and drinkers across the country. We cover the big brewers, the small brewers and everyone in between. And we'll cover the international scene with brewers not only from the United States, but also from Mexico, Canada, Australia and Europe.

The beers are listed in alphabetical order by brand name. On these pages, we will tell you what you want to know about your favorite beer, as well as a bunch of other beers. Here, we'll tell you about the history of the brand and its brewer, and the other beers that come from that brewery. We'll also talk about some interesting (and humorous) advertising and  promotional campaigns, as well as some often irrelevant, but always entertaining, trivia. Then we will spotlight some of the products that you can buy from the breweries (either in person or on-line) to show your brand loyalty (the prices we cite were current at the time of publication; actual prices may vary). You can then use this knowledge to become the king of conversation at any party!

We'd Like To Hear From You!

There could be beers on this list that you've never heard of before, and it's possible that your favorite brand didn't make it on our list. We would like to know what beers you'd put on your favorites list. Let us know what you think by logging onto our beer bulletin board at ***www.CollectorsQuest.com***.

Amstel Light

So here you are in the United States with a preference for imported beers and you are looking for a really great light beer with a full-bodied and slightly hoppy taste. Well then, Amstel Light is the beer for you. In fact, Amstel Light is the #1 imported light beer in America. And did you know that Amstel Light is available only in the United States and is imported by Heineken USA, Inc., the same people who import (you guessed it) Heineken.

This Amstel Light coaster boasts the beer's Amsterdam origin.

And Then There Was Light . . .

Introduced in 1979, Amstel Light is a fairly recent invention, but the history of the Amstel Brewery dates all the way back to 1870. That was when two Amsterdam businessmen decided to take advantage of the popularity of Bavarian beers in Holland by opening a brewery that would produce Bavarian-style lager beer. They chose to build their brewery near Amsterdam's Amstel River, so picking the beer's name seemed to flow naturally.

Yet it wasn't all that easy. As the brewing fermentation process requires ice, brewing lager beer in Holland before the days of refrigeration posed some unique problems. While this was not a problem for the Germans who used snow from the Alps or ice from Bavarian caves, the Dutch brewers had to find

> **Levity: Of The Beer And Comedic Kind**
>
> Amstel Light and "Politically Incorrect"'s Bill Maher teamed up for a 10-city road tour in 1999.

LOW CALORIE

another solution. The answer was flowing through Amsterdam's canals the whole time. It was discovered that ice could be chipped from the frozen canals in the winter and stored in double-walled cellars. So the problem was solved and by 1872, the brewery was producing 10,000 hectoliters of beer annually.

By the year 1886, the Amstel Brewery had become the largest producer of lager beer in Amsterdam. That's not a small accomplishment in a place known for pleasure. Several years earlier in 1883, Amstel had decided to share the fun and had begun exporting its beer to the United Kingdom as well

An Amstel Light bar light brightens any occasion.

as to the Dutch colonies in the Far East. By 1926, Amstel had become so popular both inside and outside of the Netherlands that it accounted for one third of the total Dutch beer exports. With a "can do" attitude

A beer tap, a familiar sight among bar-goers.

in an effort to extend its appeal, Amstel became the first Dutch brewer to export beer in cans in 1955. Then in 1969, Amstel Brewery was taken on as a subsidiary of Heineken, NV.

Among the other beers produced by the Amstel brewery are **Amstel Bock, Amstel Gold**, **Amstel Herfstbock, Amstel Lager**, **Amstel Lentebock, Amstel Malt** and **Old Bruin (Old Brown)**. Of these, only Amstel Light is currently available in the United States. Several years ago, Amstel and the pilsner-style Amstel 1870 (named for the year the brewery began operation) were briefly available in the United States, but Heineken USA stopped distributing them in 1998. It would seem that for a taste of the other beers in the Amstel stable, a trip to the Netherlands is in order.

Brew Stats

Brewer
Amstel Brewery

Location
Amsterdam, Netherlands

First Brewed
1976

Style
Lager

Taste
Full-bodied

Color
Pale gold

Alcohol Content
3.5%

The simplicity of an Amstel Light
print advertisement.

Amstel Light's advertisement
hinting at rivalry.

Amstel Advertising

Amstel Light's popular ad campaigns are often very simple, focusing on humor. At one time, Amstel Light was portrayed as "A light beer for a heavy world" in print and television advertising. A few years later, an ad campaign touted it as "the beer drinker's light beer." Other ads feature the apologetically toned slogan "In Amsterdam, we made Amstel Light taste great because we didn't know how to make it suck." Still others play upon brand rivalry.

In keeping with its sense of humor, Amstel Light sponsors events like HBO's Comedy Arts Festival in Aspen, Colorado, and the "Politically Incorrect" tour.

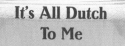

It's All Dutch To Me

Netherlands, Holland, – what's the difference? While the two names can be used interchangeably (and often are), technically, Holland only covers two regions within the Netherlands.

Hat
$7.00

Woven Blanket
$25.00

Appealing Amstel

For those whose interest in Amstel Light goes beyond mere imbibement, the official Amstel Light web site (*www.amstel-light.com*) offers a variety of stuff. Here's a sample:

T-Shirt
$10.00

Umbrella
$14.00

Sweatshirt
$28.00

Watch
$45.00

Tie
$35.00

Go to CollectorsQuest.com for more information on Amstel Light.

Anchor Steam Beer

San Francisco is known for many great things. If you're a beer lover in the Bay Area, you know that Anchor Steam Beer is a true San Francisco treat. With its unique name and its stubby-necked bottle, Anchor Steam Beer stands apart from the pack – and that's even before you pop off the teal, anchor-emblazoned bottle cap to discover a world of flavor.

Anchor Brewing Co., circa 1906.

Maytag To The Rescue

Anchor Steam Beer has been manufactured in San Francisco since 1896, but the Anchor Brewing Company enjoyed a modern renaissance in the 1960s when the company was acquired by Fritz Maytag. Washing his hands of the legendary appliance empire established by his family, Maytag devoted his time to transforming the Anchor brewery into a modern facility that turned the staid world of megabrewers on its ear. Maytag is credited with helping to inspire a new era of craft brewing that led to a resurgence in traditionally brewed premium beers. Anchor Steam Beer remains the company's standout brew, but the company also produces other brands, including **Anchor Porter**, **Liberty Ale** and **Old Foghorn** to name a few.

What's In A Name?

Perhaps Anchor Steam Beer got its name from the steam process in which it may have been originally brewed. In this process, the beer is brewed without ice, resulting in excess carbonation that looks like steam.

Letting Off Steam

The true origins of the term "steam beer" remain shrouded in mystery. Anchor Brewing Company has several theories about the origin of the term, one being that it was named for a now-lost 19th century brewing technique and another that it began with some guy named Pete Steam! Whatever the origin, Anchor Steam Beer is now made using lager yeast that is bottom fermented in shallow open fermenters instead of enclosed tanks. This unique fermentation process is often helped along by the cool air that rolls in off the San Francisco Bay.

Beer drinkers who appreciate a deep, rich flavor will wish to set sail with Anchor Steam Beer's blend of lager and ale elements that create a taste that still remains distinctive unto itself. Anchors away!

Brew Stats

Brewer
Anchor Brewing Company

Location
San Francisco, California

First Brewed
1896

Style
Steam beer

Taste
Malty, flavorful

Color
Deep amber

Alcohol Content
4.6 % (approx.)

Steaming Hot Stuff

For those of you who want to show your San Francisco style, these Anchor Steam Beer products are the way to go. Visit the Anchor Steam Brewery to purchase these items.

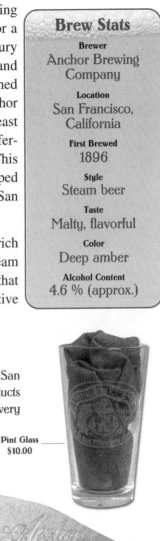

Pint Glass
$10.00

Bottle Opener
$7.25

T-Shirt
$13.50

Go to Collectors Quest.com for more information on Anchor Steam Beer.

Bass Ale

Bass Ale has a long and illustrious history, as does the brewing company that bears its name. Just take a look at some of its past. Bass Ale dates back to 1777 and is the oldest beer in the Bass Brewers family. Did you know that Bass Ale was among the beverages served on the maiden

An early Bass beer truck.

voyage of the *Titanic?* This small part of the titanic story made it into the story line of the 1996 movie about the ill-fated ocean liner, as bottles of the brew were shown among the ship's wreckage. Bass Ale is also present in several museums, as such esteemed painters as Picasso, Manet and Warhol have rendered artistic representations of this ubiquitous brew.

Brewed with its original recipe, Bass Ale is 4.4% alcohol by volume and is brewed using two strains of yeast, which, according to Bass Brewers, produce "a complex nutty, malty taste with subtle hop overtones." Bass is a cask ale, which means that it contains live yeast that continues to ferment slowly even after the beer has been bottled or casked, adding to the condition and flavor of the beer.

Mark It!

The first registered trademark in Great Britain was granted in the 1800s to Bass Brewers for the red triangle that appears as Bass Ale's logo.

Bass Ale is the leading imported draught ale and the best-selling British beer in the United States. Although it may be the best-known Bass Brewers brand in the United States, the company also produces **Caffrey's, Carling, Grolsch, Tennent's Lager** and **Worthington,** as well as

The outside of the Bass brewery..

Hooch, an alcoholic lemonade. According to Bass Brewers, their brands account for 24% of the United Kingdom beer market.

The Bass Museum

If you are interested in the history of English beer and how Bass Brewers fits into the mix, a trip to the Bass Museum located in Burton-on-Trent, Staffordshire, England, may be in order. The museum offers visitors a look at the history of Bass Brewers and of Burton-on-Trent. The Bass Museum's collection includes historic brewing equipment, pub memorabilia, photographs, vehicles and even a library of journals and brewing books. For English beer lovers, one of the highlights of a trip to the museum would be a visit to the on-premises microbrewery, which uses 18th- and 19th-century recipes from the Bass Museum archives to recreate traditional ales.

Visitors can see another aspect of the history of brewing at the Bass Museum stables. Before motor vehicles, horse-drawn wagons were the most convenient way of transporting beer. In 1900, there were 200 horses at the Bass stables. After World War I, however, Bass increasingly used motor vehicles to transport their beer, and by 1931, the number of brewery horses had diminished to just 36. Today, there are four Shire horses stabled at the Bass Museum. Their presence enables visitors to experience the grandeur and beauty of these horses, as well as learn about their role in history.

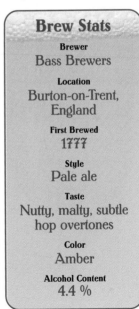

Brew Stats

Brewer
Bass Brewers

Location
Burton-on-Trent, England

First Brewed
1777

Style
Pale ale

Taste
Nutty, malty, subtle hop overtones

Color
Amber

Alcohol Content
4.4 %

Bass Ale: Legendary For A Reason

If you don't recall seeing many television ads for Bass Ale, that's because it has had a limited advertising history in the United States.

Bass premiered its first U.S. television commercial as recently as 1998. This ad campaign stars a character known as "Bass-Obsessed Man" who regales bar patrons with tales of Bass Ale in history, such as how Napoleon became so obsessed with Bass that he tried to brew it himself. These advertisements share the tagline: "Bass Ale. Legendary for a Reason." If you're interested in some more Bass Ale historical legends, check out the Bass Ale web site, *www.bassale.com*.

There is also the "Step Into The Red Triangle" campaign, which suggests that Bass is more than just a beverage, but a place you can go – perhaps a state of mind. And keeping with the notion that beer equals entertainment, Bass has sponsored "Laugh Your Bass Off!" promotions and comedy festivals at which a lucky beer-drinker and would-be comedian could win a comedy club tour in London.

"Step Into The Red Triangle" print ad.

The Bass Museum

Take a virtual trip to *www.bass-museum.com* to learn more about Bass beer, Bass Brewers and the town of Burton-on-Trent.

Bass has also teamed up with Guinness Stout on several occasions for "black and tan" promotions. A black and tan is a drink commonly made with Bass Ale and Guinness Stout. A pint glass is filled halfway with Bass (or any ale). Then Guinness (or any stout) is slowly poured over a bent spoon to fill the remainder of the glass. The two drinks will remain separated, creating a black-and-tan beverage.

Fishing For Bass Products

A trip to the Bass Museum – either in person or on-line – will introduce you to great Bass products, some of which we've shown to you below.

Hat
$20.00

Napoleon T-Shirt
$20.00

Polo Shirt
$34.00

Shackleton T-Shirt
$20.00

Bar Towel
$7.00

BASS ALE ON DRAUGHT

Bass

BREWERS OF FINE ALES SINCE 1777

Go to Collectors*Quest*.com for more information on Bass Ale.

Beck's

The history of the #1 German beer in the United States dates back more than 125 years, to a German town with a brewing history dating back to the Middle Ages. Now known as Brauerei Beck & Company, the Kaiserbrauerei Beck & May o.H.G. was founded by three men: builder Luder Rutenberg, brewmaster

A view of the Beck's brewery.

Heinrich Beck and merchant Thomas May. They selected Bremen, Germany, as their brewing location, perhaps because Bremen holds a rich brewing history. For example, one of Germany's oldest professional brewers' associations, the Bremer Brauer Societat, which dates back to 1489, calls Bremen home.

Soon after its introduction, Beck's established itself as a major export presence and was sold all over Europe and the Far East. However, the outbreaks of World War I and World War II presented obstacles to the export business. During these times, the company supported itself by providing supplies to the German troops as well as those of other European countries.

The Key To The Beck's Label

Have you been wondering why there is a key on the Beck's label? The symbol is taken from Bremen's coat of arms, and represents the key to the city.

Where's The Yeast?

Beck's is a pilsner-style beer, brewed in the 1800s and today according to the *Reinheitsgebot* – the German Purity Law of 1516. The *Reinheitsgebot* states that beer can only be brewed

An early Beck's delivery vehicle.

using malt, hops and water. (Even though yeast is an ingredient that is found in all beer, back in 1516, no one knew yeast existed – which explains why it is absent from the *Reinheitsgebot*.)

A Medal Of Excellence

It didn't take long for the quality of Beck's to be recognized, both inside and outside of Germany. In 1874, Beck's was named the best beer at the International Agricultural and Industrial Exhibition held at Bremen. Brewmaster Heinrich Beck received the Gold Medal from the German Crown Prince, who was later to become the much-loved German Emperor Friedrich III. Two years later and thousands of miles away at the World Exhibition in Philadelphia, Beck's again received a Gold Medal, this time as the best continental beer. The next time you drink a Beck's beer, take a closer look at the label and you will see representations of these medals.

Over the next few decades, Beck's wanted to reach out to new audiences. One of its strategies was to develop new styles of packaging. For example, in 1968, Brauerei Beck & Co. introduced the "Beck'ser," the company's first six-pack.

Another method of finding new audiences was to produce new products. In addition to Beck's, the company produces **Beck's Light, Beck's Dark, Beck's for Oktoberfest** (a seasonal brew available only in the United States) and **Haake Beck Non-Alcoholic.**

Beck's – The Best Of What Germans Do Best

Although Beck's has been around since 1873, its first national German advertising campaign didn't occur until 1955. Its slogan "Beck's beer quenches men's thirst" was used for about 25 years and is considered an icon in German advertising. Another longtime Beck's icon is that of a green sailing ship. It

Brew Stats

Brewer
Brauerei Beck & Co.

Location
Bremen, Germany

First Brewed
1873

Style
Pilsner

Taste
Full-bodied, hoppy

Color
Golden

Alcohol Content
4.8 %

A Beck's television advertisement.

debuted in 1984 and continues to be used today.

In the late 1990s, Beck's debuted an American advertising campaign that poked fun at German stereotypes in a lighthearted way, while pointing out what German do best – make beer. One of the spots featured a German as a stand-up comic delivering jokes in a monotone. The jokes fall flat and a voice over cuts in: "Germans don't do comedy. They do beer. Beck's. The best of what Germans do best."

Beck's also sponsors a concert whose name is a spin on Oktoberfest beer – Rocktoberfest. This concert, advertised in American rock music magazines, also features a Beck's-sponsored contest that promises a free trip to Germany to attend the performance. And keeping with the rock-and-roll theme, Beck's sponsored a recent contest in which the lucky winner would get to see the popular band Third Eye Blind in one of three cities.

A Beck's print advertisement featuring Third Eye Blind.

Recently, Beck's marketing campaigns in the United States have focused on Beck's Light and have the tagline: "All beer. No compromise." New commercials for regular Beck's feature edgy, modern music and the tagline: "Beck's. A beer apart."

Stuff That Beck's-ons You

The following items are a sample of some of the varied products that can be found on Beck's German web page at *www.becks.de.*

Baseball Cap
$8.33

T-Shirt
$12.73

Remote-Control Truck
$65.35

Travel Bag With Wheels
$34.67

Go to CollectorsQuest.com for more information on Beck's.

Black Butte Porter

The Deschutes Brewery (pronounced *day-shoots*) has only been brewing beer since 1988, but in that short span of time, its selection of beers, especially Black Butte (pronounced *byute*) Porter, have become the toast of the U.S. Pacific Northwest.

An artist's rendering of the Deschutes Brewery.

The Deschutes Brewery and Public House was the brain child of Gary Fish, a former restaurateur. Fish has said that he went into the brewery business because the booming success of brew pubs nationally made it an amazing opportunity and a worthy risk. With input from his father, a veteran of the wine industry, and a friend, a veteran brewer, Fish had the necessary brain power and experience needed to make his dream a reality.

Fish named his Bend, Oregon, brewery after the rapidly moving Deschutes River located nearby. The brewery soon took on the pace of its namesake, and quickly began winning over beer drinkers.

Deschutes has also been winning awards at an equally fast pace. In 1999, it was voted "Brewpub of the Year" at the Third Annual National Brewpub Conference & Tradeshow. The brewery's celebrated Black Butte Porter has won seven medals in beer competitions including four gold medal wins. These gold medals have been awarded at the NABA Competition

Phenomenal Growth

What started as a single brew pub producing about 300 barrels in its first year has expanded into a full-fledged brewery that produces about 80,000 barrels annually.

(twice), the California Brewers Festival and the Great American Beer Festival.

Deschutes also brews **Bachelor ESB, Cascade Ale, Mirror Pond Pale Ale** and **Obsidian Stout.** It has several seasonal offerings, including **Broken Top Bock, Jubelale, Pine Mountain Pils** and **Quail Springs IPA.**

Black Butte Porter is not only a favorite of the critics, but is the peoples' choice as well. In addition to being a medal winner, Black Butte Porter is the top-selling porter throughout the U.S. Pacific Northwest.

A Real Beaut

Show your loyalty to Black Butte Porter by wearing clothing promoting the brand and by drinking your favorite porter out of customized glassware. Visit *www.deschutesbrewery.com* for more!

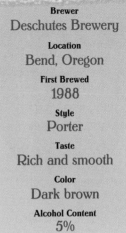

Brew Stats

Brewer
Deschutes Brewery

Location
Bend, Oregon

First Brewed
1988

Style
Porter

Taste
Rich and smooth

Color
Dark brown

Alcohol Content
5%

Black Butte Porter

Pint Glass
$3.00

Mug
$8.00

Hat
$12.00

T-Shirt
$15.00

Go to Collectors Quest.com for more information on Black Butte Porter.

Bud Light

When "light" beers burst onto the brewing scene, many so-called beer experts and consumers predicted they were merely a passing trend. Bud Light has proved the naysayers wrong. Although Bud Light may have started out in this so-called "niche" market,

The Anheuser-Busch Brewery in St. Louis, Missouri.

the brand has emerged as not only the nation's #1 light beer, but also the #2 beer overall, second only to big brother Budweiser. Bud Light has become so ingrained in the culture that one of the popular lager's recent television ads portrayed Bud Light as more essential than *toilet paper*.

Rising To The Top

Believe it or not, Bud Light was *not* Anheuser-Busch's first reduced-calorie beer on the market – that honor goes to Natural Light, which started appearing on store shelves in 1977. Originally named Budweiser Light, the beer was first test-marketed in April of 1981, and one year later it was introduced to the entire United States.

Budweiser Light had a tough go of it at first. It faced stiff competition in the marketplace from Lite Beer from Miller, which had an almost decade-long head start in attracting customers to light beer. However, the smooth, cool and refreshing flavor and overall un-"light" taste of

"The Boys Night Out"

The handsome foursome from the "Ladies Night" commercials became so popular that they went on to record a CD of classic rock songs entitled "The Boys Night Out."

Budweiser Light began to win over beer drinkers who did not normally drink light beer and convert light beer drinkers who had previously consumed other brands.

Budweiser Light has undergone few changes over the years in its march to the top. One major change worth noting is the change of the beer's name. In 1984, the beer shortened its name to the more-familiar Bud Light. Its early advertising slogan of

An early Budweiser Light can.

"Bring out your best" was replaced by the "Gimme a light . . . no, Bud Light" ads, which not only helped to solidify the brand's new name, but also helped the brand to distinguish itself from its competitors.

Spuds Mackenzie & Friends

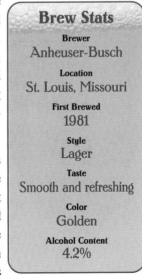

Spuds Mackenzie figurine.

Bud Light continued to gain market share after its debut. With the debut of pitchman, er, pitch*dog* Spuds Mackenzie in the late 1980s, the brand would see its sales increase even more. Spuds, a bull terrier, was an advertising and marketing phenomenon. Often seen sporting sunglasses and a gaudy shirt, Spuds was usually surrounded by a bevy of beautiful women. Spuds was the popular star of several Bud Light ads, and appeared on a wide variety of merchandise. Spuds, however, became quite controversial, as many of his fans included children and other underage drinkers. The advertising campaign featuring him was soon abandoned.

While no singular ad campaign since has achieved the notoriety that Spuds Mackenzie did, Bud Light has aired several in recent years that are truly memorable. Among Bud Light's most popular characters through the years are the group of guys who dress up in women's clothes to score free Bud Lights

Brew Stats

Brewer
Anheuser-Busch

Location
St. Louis, Missouri

First Brewed
1981

Style
Lager

Taste
Smooth and refreshing

Color
Golden

Alcohol Content
4.2%

Bud Light television advertisements.

from bars holding "Ladies Night" promotions. One recent ad, featuring a guy who uses a goggle-wearing mouse to scare a pretty neighbor into bringing her Bud Light over to his house, elicits laughs due to its off-the-wall humor. So does the spot in which a man ignores his date's request to look out for her "cat" in the kitchen – a cat who turns out to be a full-size tiger protecting the Bud Light from strangers.

Anheuser-Busch ads have become a much-anticipated tradition during the annual Super Bowl telecast. Several spots, such as the series of Bud Bowl commercials, have seemingly made their mark on *football* history, let alone advertising history. The "Paper or Plastic?" ad featuring two shoppers who have a tough time deciding whether to buy Bud Light or toilet paper with the last of their meager funds was another laugh-inducing Super Bowl spot.

Aloha

Have you seen the special "Aloha" label that appears on selected bottles of Bud Light? The labels feature an outline of the Hawaiian islands. "Aloha" means hello and goodbye, and these bottles sure are a *good buy.*

From the "Yes I am" guy who will admit to being anybody when he sees an opportunity to get a free Bud Light, to Johnny, the guy who made "I love you, man" a household phrase, Anheuser-Busch has been able to carefully craft an image for Bud Light that is both youthful and humorous.

Endorsement Superstars

Bud Light continues to lure some of the best and brightest stars in music, sports and entertainment to help sell its

Bud Light clock.

product. Bud Light celebrities are not afraid to laugh at themselves or poke fun at their fame. Country singer Tim McGraw has starred in several commercials that take a wry look at the perils of celebrity. One commercial has McGraw being recognized by fans not for his musical accomplishments, but for being married to the beautiful and talented singer Faith Hill. Another commercial has McGraw being admired not for his music, but for his good looks.

Wayne Gretzky, hockey's "Great One," has also teamed up with Bud Light in his role as commissioner of the mock Bubble Boys Hockey League. Gretzky, the National Hockey League's all-time leading scorer, signed on with Bud Light in 1999. His spots have aired on radio and television, and print advertisements have also appeared.

Women make up a significant portion of light beer drinkers and Bud Light does not neglect this important segment of consumers. Commercials starring notable female athletes such as World Cup soccer champion Julie Foudy, who humorously practices her soccer skills with a head of cabbage in the supermarket, appeal to several demographic categories.

Bud Light neon sign.

The Bud Bowl Lives On

In 1994, Bud Light reached an extraordinary pinnacle. Just 12 years after its national introduction, it became the best-selling light beer in the United States. With America's continued thirst for light beers, it's speculated that Bud Light might soon overtake Budweiser as the #1 beer overall – it's almost as if the fictional Bud Bowl competition has come to life!

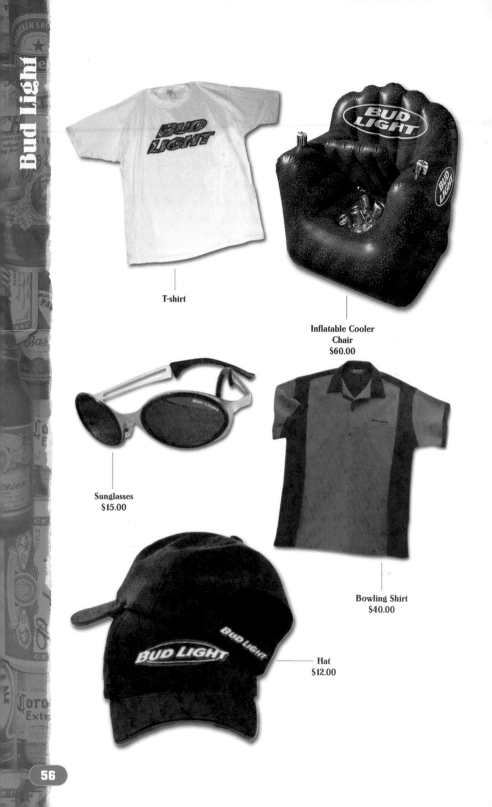

T-shirt

Inflatable Cooler
Chair
$60.00

Sunglasses
$15.00

Bowling Shirt
$40.00

Hat
$12.00

T-Shirt
$12.00

Party Girl Hat
$16.00

Gimme A Light!

It's easy to demonstrate your enthusiasm for Bud Light with all of the great products available from *www.bud-shop.com*. Products with out prices are available only at promotional events.

Ski Biscuit
$99.00

Go to CollectorsQuest.com for more information on Bud Light.

Budweiser

There's a reason why Budweiser is called the "King Of Beers." Since its debut in 1876, Budweiser has been the beer that sets the standard for all other American lagers. There are probably not

The Budweiser brewery.

too many people who would argue that among all the U.S. beers available today, Budweiser deserves the crown and throne.

Budweiser's original home is the Anheuser-Busch brewery in St. Louis, Missouri. The brewery was first known as the Bavarian Brewery and was owned by Eberhard Anheuser. Adolphus Busch came into the picture in 1864 when he married Anheuser's daughter, Lilly. Busch also began working at the Bavarian Brewery. Twelve years later, in 1876, the Bavarian Brewery was renamed the Anheuser-Busch brewery, in recognition of Busch's tremendous efforts in moving the company to the forefront of U.S. beer brewers.

Budweiser's Bow Tie

Budweiser's familiar "bow tie" logo, which is found in advertisements, neon signs and other visible locations, debuted in 1956.

The Budweiser brand was the result of efforts by Busch and his friend Carl Conrad to produce a beer similar in flavor to a beer that they had found and enjoyed in the German town of Ceske Budejovice. The Anheuser-Busch

Adolphus Busch

brewery took a gamble that the new "Budweiser" beer would be a success – and. luckily for all Bud lovers, it was right!

In addition to the well-known Budweiser brands (which include **Bud Light, Bud Ice, Bud Ice Light** and **Bud Dry), Busch** and **Busch Light** and **Natural Light** products, Anheuser-Busch also brews the microbrew **Red Wolf,** and the non-alcoholic brands **O'Doul's** and **O'Doul's Amber.**

Budweiser Means More Than Just Beer

Budweiser hasn't become a successful product, however, just because it tastes good. There are other variables responsible for creating a successful product. For example, production and shipping methods play a role, as do advertising and marketing techniques. This combination of resources has helped to make the words "beer" and "Budweiser" almost synonymous in the minds of many beer drinkers.

One rather accidental marketing technique is the Budweiser Clydesdales. These beautiful horses, long associated with Anheuser-Busch and with Budweiser in particular, date back to 1933. The Clydesdales

Brew Stats

Brewer
Anheuser-Busch

Location
St. Louis, Missouri

First Brewed
1876

Style
Lager

Taste
Smooth and crisp

Color
Golden

Alcohol Content
4.9% (approx.)

A typical scene in the Clydesdales' stable as depicted in a figurine.

had been a gift from August A. Busch Jr. to his father to commemorate the repeal of Prohibition. These immense and noble animals instantly became a popular attraction, and today the Budweiser Clydesdales regularly travel 100,000 miles a year in their role as ambassadors of Budweiser.

Another way Anheuser-Busch promotes itself is by producing an almost limitless variety of Budweiser collectibles for budgets both big and small. Cold-cast porcelain Clydesdale figurines are available in both open and limited numbered editions. Handcrafted steins are a popular collectible that are meant to be displayed, not actually used. There are also solid brass coins, pewter eggs, train sets and metal cars and trucks just waiting to be collected. You can place Budweiser ornaments on your Christmas tree. There's even a die-cast blimp!

Getting The Word Out

Ever since Anheuser-Busch's earliest days, advertising has played a significant role in increasing Budweiser's visibility and influence across the United States, and later, the world.

In the early 1900s, Anheuser-Busch successfully marketed its Budweiser brand as an alternative to more potent alcoholic drinks through memorable advertising campaigns. Early print ads featuring patriotic images of George Washington and explorer Leif Ericsson stressed that "Budweiser Means Moderation."

Frogs, Ferrets And Lizards, Oh My!

The Budweiser lizards.

Budweiser has been riding a wave of popularity thanks to strong commercials that have a way of ingraining themselves in the public mind. No one could doubt the appeal of frogs, ferres and lizards as advertising pitchmen after these four-legged creatures helped turn around Budweiser's image as a beer for older, more conservative drinkers. The animals professing their love of Budweiser spawned a long-running (and ongoing) television campaign.

A catch phrase that has recently become even more ubiquitous than "Bud-weis-er" is the "Whassup!" that is featured in a series of

"Whassup!" has become a catch phrase for Budweiser drinkers and non-drinkers alike.

commercials and merchandise. Rather than featuring the celebrities and athletes who frequently appear in beer ads, these spots portray friends simply hanging out and enjoying their favorite beer. These ad spots have proven to be successful, as the original "Whassup!" commercial received the renowned Grand Clio award, the pinnacle of achievement in the advertising world. If imitation is said to be the sincerest form of flattery, the "Whassup!" ads should feel very flattered. Parodies of this advertising campaign abound.

And who can forget Bud Man? This "Dauntless Defender of Quality" made his debut in 1969, and recently had his super-heroics honored with an official Anheuser-Busch 30th anniversary stein. Budweiser fans can sleep soundly at night knowing that their beer is protected as long as Bud Man is on patrol.

Courtesy of Dan Morean

Bud Man defends quality.

Budweiser has also been the recipient of successful catch phrases. Everyone knows "This Bud's for you!" or has been told "Nothing beats a Bud" or "Proud to be your Bud."

Budweiser Joins The Team

Budweiser is a part of the sporting landscape around the globe, and no bigger sporting arena exists than the millions of

Budweiser sponsors Dale Earnhardt Jr. in the Winston Cup races.

"Born on date" on a Budweiser bottle.

households that watch the Super Bowl on television each January. The Super Bowl has become well known for its memorable commercials. Today, a 30-second Super Bowl commercial may run upwards of $3 million. Anheuser-Busch regularly purchases ten such spots.

Budweiser has closely aligned itself with the athletic world in many other ways as well. It recently teamed up with NASCAR phenomenon Dale Earnhardt Jr. as the primary sponsor of his Winston Cup efforts. Budweiser also embraces sports on the world stage, and is the official beer sponsor for soccer's FIFA World Cup Tournament.

Freshness And The Future

Sports promotions and clever commercials can only get a company so far. Budweiser would not be in the leadership position it is if the beer was no good. As they have 12 regional breweries, allowing for the continuous shipment of only the freshest beer, Anheuser-Busch began adding "Born On" dates to Budweiser to assure consumers of the freshness of their Budweiser.

Millennium Budweiser can.

Part of Budweiser's success is that it has not strayed far from its roots. By avoiding trends and fads in packaging and design, Budweiser exists in a class all its own. A Budweiser bottle from 1890 looks very similar to a bottle from 1990, and that's likely to continue for the next 100 years. Despite all the hype surrounding the new millennium, Budweiser stayed traditional and introduced subtle millennium graphics on cans and bottles of Budweiser.

Whether you're enjoying your Budweiser from a longneck bottle at a trendy bar or straight from the can on a hot summer day, Budweiser remains the American standard of quality and excellence in lager beer.

Bud Buys

Leapin' lizards! There are a lot of swell Budweiser products. Visit the Budweiser store on the Internet at *www.budshop.com* to find out more.

Neon Clock
$69.00

Cooler
$110.00

Dalmatian Stein
$40.00

Lizard Denim
Shirt
$50.00

Foldable Chair
$45.00

Ferret Stein
$29.50

Golf Bag
$130.00

Mesh Shorts
$31.00

Tractor Trailer
$45.00

Label Swimsuit
$40.00

Bow Tie
Beach Towel
$10.00

Inflatable
Cooler Couch
$95.00

Lizard Hat
$9.00

Fleece Pants
$29.00

Go to CollectorsQuest.com for more
information on Budweiser.

Busch

When you open a can or bottle of Busch and hear the *whoosh* of the carbonation escaping, you can't help but be transported to the icy, rocky mountain top depicted on the Busch label. The familiar Busch mountain design has appeared on its

The main Anheuser-Busch brewery in St. Louis, Missouri.

cans and bottles ever since the brand's inception in 1955 and has remained to the present day.

Heading To The Mountains

The mountains have always played an important role in Busch's advertising campaigns. An early ad invited drinkers to "Discover Bavaria – in a glass" with the snow-capped mountains in the background. Later campaigns suggested that Busch beer drinkers "head for the mountains" as they enjoy the cool refreshment of Busch.

Busch's appreciation for the outdoors runs deeper than just the icy-cold mountaintop in their advertisements. The recent "Busch Blue Waters" campaign benefitted American Rivers, an organization dedicated to river protection and conservation. In this campaign, consumers submitted photographs of particular bodies of water. The photos deemed as best portraying that body of water were made into Busch billboards. A $1,500 prize was award-

30,000 Cans Of Beer On The Wall!

More than 30,000 cans of Busch line the walls of a home near the University of Cincinnati campus. The cans have been saved by house residents (college students) since 1984.

66

ed to both the winning photographers and American Rivers, who shared their portion with local conservation groups.

An early coaster showing the Busch Bavarian name.

Famed wildlife imitator Wayne Carlton is a Busch spokesperson who brings the sounds of the rugged outdoors right through your radio. His talent for reproducing various animal calls has earned him the respect of outdoorsmen throughout North America and is highlighted in his radio spots for Busch.

A Return To Bavarian Roots

For almost 50 years now, beer drinkers have been enjoying Busch. It was created by Anheuser-Busch in 1955 and was sold at the time under the name of "Busch Bavarian." (Budweiser, Anheuser-Busch's flagship brand, has been brewed since 1876.) Anheuser-Busch began production of this popularly priced beer in part to ensure that their brewing facilities maintained production at full capacity and to fill gaps in the Budweiser brewing and bottling schedule. Busch Bavarian was originally test-marketed in just 16 states. It met with a favorable response and accounted for 2% of the beer that Anheuser-Busch produced at the time.

Busch Bavarian grew steadily and, by 1965, it established a significant foothold in the market, accounting for 15% of all beer consumed in the United States. By 1978, Busch Bavarian was ready for national distribution. Its packaging received a facelift and its name was shortened to Busch.

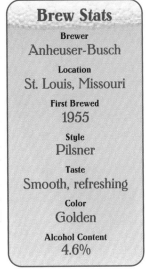

Brew Stats

Brewer
Anheuser-Busch

Location
St. Louis, Missouri

First Brewed
1955

Style
Pilsner

Taste
Smooth, refreshing

Color
Golden

Alcohol Content
4.6%

A Growing Family

The Busch family of beers currently includes Busch, **Busch Light** and **Busch Ice.** Since 1994, the taste of Busch has been reproduced in a non-alcoholic beverage known as **Busch NA. Busch Light Draft** and **Busch Cold-Filtered Draft** have also become available in select test markets. While not all of these products have caught on nationally, they remain important trailblazers in the development of future Busch beers.

An early Busch Bavarian can.

Roll Out The Barrels

The annual production of the Busch family of beers now exceeds seven million barrels. Busch has experienced a renaissance as a result of an increased commitment by Anheuser-Busch to budgeting, advertising and marketing the brand. The image of Busch beer has evolved from the rich tradition of Bavarian beer brewing to the appealing lure of clean, mountain refreshment.

Anheuser-Busch is currently the largest brewer in the United States. The company that today maintains 12 domestic breweries and produces over 30 different beverages, including the Busch, **Budweiser** and **Michelob** brands, has its roots in two men who, even in the company's earliest days, thirsted for their tasty beers to dominate the country.

Who Were Anheuser And Busch?

Making an early Anheuser-Busch beer delivery.

Eberhard Anheuser was a prosperous soap manufacturer in St. Louis, Missouri, who acquired the struggling Bavarian Brewery, a local business that had been brewing beer since 1852. The brewery continued under Anheuser's stewardship, but its true success came with

Two sides of a Busch coaster.

Adolphus Busch, another German who had been brewing beer in Missouri since his immigration in 1857. After he married Lilly Anheuser, Eberhard's daughter, in 1861, Busch became a partner in his father-in-law's business. He took over as president following Anheuser's death in 1880.

Since then, the family-owned company has continued to pave the way in the beer marketplace with aggressive marketing techniques and technological innovations.

In The Driver's Seat

The Anheuser-Busch name has become a familiar one to sports fans, especially through its sponsorship of NASCAR. Busch's involvement began in 1978, when Anheuser-Busch sponsored the Busch Pole Award in the Winston Cup series. That sponsorship was followed by the Busch Clash, now known as the Bud Shootout.

Since 1984, Busch has lent its name to the NASCAR Busch Series, Grand National Division. Anheuser-Busch began its involvement with the series in 1982, which was then known as the NASCAR Budweiser Late Model Sportsman Series. The Busch circuit has become the premier place to catch both rising stars and established veterans of the track. Successful drivers such as Jeff Gordon and Dale Earnhardt Jr. have all learned the ropes of stock car racing in the competitive Busch series.

Take A Tour!

Seven Anheuser-Busch breweries across the country are available for touring. Choose from the following: Fairfield, Calif.; Fort Collins, Colo.; Jacksonville, Fla.; St. Louis, Mo.; Merrimack, N.H.; Columbus, Ohio and Williamsburg, Va.

Off To The Races Or The Mountaintop

You can tell the world your love for Busch either by showing off your Busch racing or Busch beer paraphernalia. For more information, visit *www.budshop.com.*

T-Shirt
(front and back shown)
$12.00

Hat
$9.00

Hat
$14.00

Button-down Shirt
$54.00

T-Shirt
$10.50

Hand Towel
$0.99

T-Shirt
$10.50

Pool Cue
$4.95

Hat
$9.00

VICTORINOX
SWISS ARMY EQUIPPED

BUSCH BEER

Army Knife
$16.00

Go to CollectorsQuest.com for more
information on Busch.

71

Busch Light

Natural Light might have been the first, and Bud Light might be the best-selling, but Busch Light has also made its mark as one of Anheuser-Busch's reduced-calorie favorites.

A view of the Anheuser-Busch brewery in St. Louis, Missouri.

Newcomer To The Scene

Even though Busch Light was first introduced in 1990, it didn't complete its U.S. introductions until 1998, when the markets of California and Nevada received their first distribution of Busch Light. When the Busch family of beers started out, they were intended to be solely Midwest regional brands. However, they have now become a brand name familiar to beer drinkers from coast to coast.

Busch Light's affordable price and smooth taste has helped make it one of the top 10 beer brands in the country, and it continues to hold its market share. Busch Light has been able to retain its loyal customers while gaining new fans every day, including Busch Light drinkers in Canada.

Brew Stats

Brewer
Anheuser-Busch

Location
St. Louis, Missouri

First Brewed
1990

Style
Pilsner

Taste
Crisp, smooth

Color
Golden

Alcohol Content
4.2%

Racing To The Great Outdoors

Not only is Busch Light a proud sponsor of NASCAR (in association with Anheuser-Busch's Busch racing series), but the brand has also sponsored its own races. In 1994, 1995 and 1996, Busch

Light sponsored NASCAR-level races at the Atlanta Motor Speedway. Driver Terry Labonte won the Busch Light 300 in 1996, the same year he became Winston Cup champion.

Have you seen Busch Light's commemorative racing cans? The Great Tracks Commemorative Can promotion featured several well-known NASCAR race tracks, including Bristol Motor Speedway and Atlanta Motor Speedway.

Busch Light coaster.

Busch and Busch Light magazine ad.

Racing isn't the only thing that comes to mind when one thinks "Busch Light." With its catch-phrase "Head for the mountains," Busch Light is a beverage associated with sportsmen and nature lovers, and recent advertising promotions have captured that crisp outdoor feeling.

Gear Up For The Mountains

Prepare for your trip to the mountains with these Busch Light products!

Hat
$10.00

Key Chain/
Bottle Opener
$0.50

T-Shirt
$9.00

Go to CollectorsQuest.com for more information on Busch Light.

Coors

You don't need any more reason to drink Original Coors than I "feel like it." In fact, it's not just *people* who crave the cold, clean taste of Coors. It seems to be popular among space aliens as well, as movie viewers may remember E.T.'s amusing

A look at the Coors Brewery.

encounter with Coors beer in Steven Spielberg's production.

The reason E.T. was able to drink Coors back in 1982 is that his spaceship left him stranded in California. Had E.T. been marooned on the East Coast he probably wouldn't have found any Coors in the refrigerator, since Coors was originally available only in the western United States at the time. Although Coors did initially cross the Mississippi in 1981, the beer was not readily available throughout the nation until 1991.

Go West, Young Man

The Coors Brewery in Golden, Colorado, was founded in 1873 by Adolph Coors, a German immigrant. He learned the brewing trade when at 14, he entered into a three-year apprenticeship agreement at the Henry Wenker Brewery in the city of Dortmund, Germany.

Once the apprenticeship ended, Coors remained an employee until he was 21. But he was an ambitious man and the political and economic climate in Germany persuaded him to

Fit For A President

Former President Gerald Ford was known to return to the White House from his second home in Colorado with several cases of Coors.

The golden color of Coors.

travel to the United States. So he set forth on an adventure, stowing away on a ship bound for the United States, arriving penniless and jobless in Baltimore, Maryland, in 1868. Coors stayed in Baltimore to work for a while and then began to make his way west as the region promised opportunity. On his way, Coors worked a variety of jobs from brick-layer to common laborer.

In 1869, he arrived in Naperville, Illinois, where he returned to the brewing business after landing a job as foreman of the Stenger Brewery. However, feeling that the country had more to offer, Adolph left the brewery two-and-a-half years later, moving on to Denver, Colorado.

He bought himself a partnership in a bottling company, then bought out his partner by the end of the year. One of his bottling customers was Jacob Schueler, who teamed up with Adolph to open The Golden Brewery in 1873. By 1880, Adolph was able to buy out Schueler and soon after changed the name to Coors Brewery. A quick success, the brewery's annual output by 1890 was 17,600 barrels (at 31 gallons each), and the company was truly golden.

Brew Stats

Brewer
Coors Brewing Company

Location
Golden, Colorado

First Brewed
1873

Style
Lager

Taste
Crisp, clean

Color
Golden

Alcohol Content
5.0%

Prohibition And Beyond

Catastrophe struck in 1916, when the Colorado outlawed alcohol production. The Coors Brewery had to struggle through Prohibition four years longer than breweries in other parts of the country. While the company tried its hand at marketing a near-beer called Mannah, it had more success with another non-alcoholic product – malted milk. So once again demonstrating its keen sense of business acumen, Coors survived Prohibition.

After Prohibition, the company went full steam ahead to expand its U.S. presence. To begin with, Coors expanded its market to encompass 11 Western states.

Coors continued brewing through World War II, with half of its output reserved for soldiers (since the government, in a complete reversal of its anti-alcohol stance of the 1920s, now considered beer vital for soldier morale). Coors' wartime beer had a lower alcohol content than that which was brewed during peacetime. Since demand exceeded supply, lower alcohol concentrations allowed for the pro-duction of more beer.

Non-alcoholic Coors.

All this time Coors had been a purely regional beer (not counting their export to soldiers in wartime), and they only produced one product, Original Coors Banquet Beer. In the 1970s, the company began to change aspects of this, both by expanding into new markets, further extending its reach. In addition to being available throughout the United States, Coors is now available in

This coaster foretells Coors' expansion.

approximately 40 international mar-kets. Coors also introduced a new product – **Coors Light,** which debuted in 1978. Today Coors markets about 20 different brands, an impressive statistic when considering that the company did not even "go national" until 1991. They've received acclaim for their other brews, which include **Blue Moon Belgian White**, **Keystone**, **Killian Irish Red** and **Zima**.

Rocky Mountain High

Coors has always been proud of its Colorado heritage, and this pride is evidenced in the packaging and marketing of Coors. Cans and bottles of Coors are emblazoned with the words "Brewed in Golden, Colorado, with Rocky Mountain water." The company also touts its Rocky Mountain heritage with a package blurb that informs

Coors drinkers that Coors has been brewed at an altitude of 5,687 feet (about a mile high) for over 120 years, and that it's the location and ingredients that make all the difference in brewing a great beer.

It should come as no surprise, then, that these same attributes have been the focus of several Coors advertising campaigns. In 1994, Coors launched a campaign that praised the beer as being cold and clean and the one to drink because "you feel like it." These radio and television ads played up the spirit of the West, spinning tales of unique characters and their adventures.

In a 1994 Denver Post article, the Coors brand manager was quoted as saying, "Coors advertising was designed to be different. Its quirky but provocative style is intended to appeal to consumers who identify with the independent spirit of the West and the brand's Rocky Mountain heritage. The ads tell stories about interesting people you would like to drink beer with." A 1998 ad played up the brand's location, emphasizing that "there's only one mile-high taste."

Savings In A Can

Coors pioneered the use of aluminum cans in packaging, introducing this packaging on January 22, 1959. Coors also instituted an early recycling program, offering customers a penny for every can returned.

An Original Coors delivery van.

And probably everyone has seen the ads that persuade beer drinkers to "tap the rockies." In one in particular, a thirsty male club-goer inadvertently responds in all the wrong ways to his sexy female friend – because he's following a waitress' tray of Coors. The moral of the story: Coors is so appealing that it can even manage to distract a person from the charms of a beautiful woman.

Cap
$19.00

Recycle Bin
$26.00

Of Coors, I'll Buy It

You can bring a bit of the Rockies into your own home with Coors products from stylish caps to recycle bins. To see what you can get, visit *www.coors.com.*

Neon Clock
$72.00

Pewter Logo Mug
$12.00

1947 Pickup
Truck Bank
$40.00

Woven Blanket
$50.00

125th
Anniversary Stein
$39.00

Can Holder
$3.50

Playing Cards
$2.50

Go to CollectorsQuest.com for more
information on Coors.

Coors Light

So you have been hit by "The Silver Bullet," and it feels pretty good. Coors Light, which debuted in 1978 and is commonly known as "The Silver Bullet" due to its silver packaging, was introduced at a time when light beers were growing in popularity and

Coors Light is a popular beverage.

Coors was looking to expand its market presence. It was originally introduced in the same camel-colored can as Original Coors, but was eventually repackaged in a flashy silver can. With this new marketing scheme, Coors Light took a shot that hit its mark. And today, it accounts for approximately 70% of Coors' business.

Not Just A Shot In The Dark

"The Silver Bullet" was the first new product to be introduced in the company's then 105-year history. Up until 1978, Coors was a regional company, selling Original Coors in 11 states in the western United States. Coors had acquired a certain mystique, however, and those living in the East were often eager to get their hands on it.

In Touch With The Feminine Side

In the late 1980s, Coors reminded women that "you don't have to be a man to appreciate great beer," with ads in female-targeted magazines.

In 1981, soon after Coors Light was introduced, distribution of Coors crossed the Mississippi River. As Coors' distribution grew, so did the popularity of Coors Light. Over the next decade, Coors grew from a regional company to a national presence, and by 1991

Coors Light coasters in their distinctive silver color.

Coors was the third-largest brewer in the United States and was experiencing the industry's fastest volume growth rate. Coors has since gone international with products now being sold in over 30 markets around the world.

Coors Light, which became the company's #1 brand nine years after it was introduced, played a major role in the phenomenal growth of the company and still contributes to its success. Other company success stories include **Coors Extra Gold**, **Original Coors** and **Winterbrew** (a seasonal beer); the **Keystone** and **Killian's** lines and **Blue Moon**, Coors' line of specialty beers.

Why is "The Silver Bullet" so popular? Coors' Senior V.P. of Marketing, Bill Weintraub, pondered this in a "Denver Rocky Mountain News" article, asking, "What is it about Coors Light that is special and important and distinct? It's Rocky Mountain refreshment. It's a very refreshing, drinkable product." Perhaps therein lies the answer and it's that simple – part taste, part "Coors mystique."

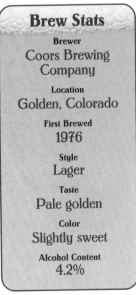

Brew Stats

Brewer
Coors Brewing Company

Location
Golden, Colorado

First Brewed
1976

Style
Lager

Taste
Pale golden

Color
Slightly sweet

Alcohol Content
4.2%

Tap The Rockies

Besides the quality of the brand – Coors Light won a gold medal in the American-style light lager category at the 1998 Great American Beer Festival – the unique and memorable advertising of Coors Light has contributed a great deal to the brand's success.

A recent series of commercials, known as the "Beer Man" spots, in which a male beer vendor (and later, an attractive female vendor) becomes the center of attention because of his frosty brews for sale, has proven to be very popular with consumers. The gender switch was made because a young, attractive and beer-knowledge-able woman was though to be more appealing than an older, overweight, male beer vendor.

Coors hasn't had a short-age of celebrity endorsers. TV spots covered themes that incorporated old John Wayne movie footage in which the legendary actor seems to inter-act with Coors Light drinkers and play football with former NFL star Howie Long. Do you

A coaster depicting two bar favorites – Coors Light and pool.

remember the ad in which former "Cheers" star George Wendt runs across a stadium to the romantic song lyrics "Just like me, they long to be, close to you . . ." in the background? He is reaching for some-thing off the screen, and then you see it: the beer man. And then there is the romantic moment when Wendt meets his ideal object of beauty: a Coors Light.

Of course you remember the "Tap The Rockies" series of adver-tisements, which played upon the use of icy-cold Rocky Mountain water in Coors Light. This campaign had peo-ple humming the "Tap the Rockies" jingle and made everyone aware that Coors Light is "frost-brewed Rocky Mountain refreshment."

Coors Light television advertisement.

The ice-cold theme runs rampant in Coors Light advertising. Print ads show a frosty can just dripping with con-densation. You may recall the TV ad in which a woman tells her per-spiring boyfriend that he's "getting colder" in his search for the shirt she's hidden. As he opens the door of a refrigerator filled with cold Coors Light she tells him he's "ice cold." Commercials for Coors

A lighted bottle-cap sign.

Light are also jumping into the technological era with computer themes in a series of "dot.cold" ads

One of the most notable sponsorships undertaken by Coors Light is that of the all-female baseball team, the Silver Bullets. Born in 1993 and managed by Phil Niekro, a Hall of Fame pitcher, this team toured the country, competing against all-men's amateur teams.

Coors Tours

If the world of Coors Light seen through television and print ads isn't enough for you and you would you like to take a look behind the scenes to see where Coors Light is made, then you may want to take a tour. The Coors Brewing Company offers daily tours at their primary brewery in Golden, Colo., which take visitors through the entire brewing process, from malting to brewing to packaging. After the tour, refresh yourself with a complementary beer sample or soft drink. The tour also includes a stop at the Coors And Company gift shop. Brewery tours are open to all, but visitors under 18 must be accompanied by an adult. For more information, call (303) 277-BEER.

A Coors Light neon sign.

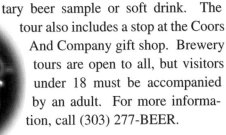

Coors Light on tap – yet another bar fave.

Par For The Coors

You can find almost anything from a dart set to a beverage belt with a Coors Light logo at *www.coors.com*. Products without prices are available only at promotional events.

Beverage Belt
$16.00

Beach Towel
$18.00

Cap
$15.00

Cooler
$28.00

Dart Set
$16.00

Ladies' Baseball
Shirt
$18.00

Mug (set of four)
$15.00

Golf Cap
$12.00

Logo Mirror
$35.00

Sweatshirt
$40.00

Key Chain/
Bottle Opener

Go to CollectorsQuest.com for more
information on Coors Light.

Corona Extra

What do you get when you cross "fun in the sun, warm hospitality, relaxation and good times," Jimmy Buffet and beer? Why, Corona Extra, the #1-selling imported beer in the United States, of course.

A coaster for the Cinco de Mayo promotion.

Corona Extra had its beginnings in 1925 when the Mexican company Grupo Modelo founded a brewery in Mexico City called La Cervecería Modelo. Seventy-five years later, Corona Extra is not only Grupo Modelo's flagship brand, but also the #1-selling beer in Mexico, the #1-selling export in the United States and the fifth-best selling beer in the world!

Corona Extra had a banner year in 1997, when its sales surpassed those of Heineken. This event made Corona the largest-selling imported beer in the United States, and marked the first time an import brand other than Heineken had held the #1 spot since Prohibition was repealed all the way back in 1933!

Corona Extra Around The Globe

Don't worry about a lack of Corona Extra if you're traveling around the globe. The beer is available in North and South America, Europe, Asia and Africa.

Corona Extra Crosses The Border . . .

Despite its huge popularity in Mexico, Corona Extra didn't make its way over the border into the United States until 1978. This is when Grupo Modelo created an international division and hired Barton Beers, Ltd. to distribute this Mexican taste in the western United States. The beer was an instant success in states like Texas and California, and within eight years, Corona Extra had become the second-best selling imported beer in the United States, second only to Heineken.

A blow-up plane advertising the "Island Shuttle" promotion depicts Corona's philosophy of fun and relaxation.

By this time, Grupo Modelo had hired importers to distribute Corona in the eastern United States, where it quickly challenged the top imports in popularity. Proving that style is everything, Corona's success was tied in large part to the status-symbol image imported beers enjoyed among young urban professionals.

. . . And Then, Crosses Many Others

With the increasing growth of Corona's popularity, the last thing that Grupo Modelo could do was indulge in some laid-back relaxation it was so successful in promoting. Eager to keep building the brand, in 1986 Grupo Modelo created a subsidiary to work with importers, protect brand trademarks and play a dominant role in promoting and merchandising Corona Extra in the international marketplace.

In the 1990s, Grupo Modelo developed affiliates in Belgium, Spain, Singapore and Costa Rica to oversee distribution and marketing efforts in Europe, the Middle East, Africa, Asia and Central and South America.

Although Corona Extra is Grupo Modelo's most popular brand, it is not the only beer that the company brews or exports. In addition to Corona Extra and **Corona Light**, Grupo Modelo also exports **Negra Modelo**, **Modelo Especial** and **Pacifico Clara**. And they seem to have a cor-

Brew Stats

Brewer
Grupo Modelo

Location
Mexico City, Mexico

First Brewed
1925

Style
Lager

Taste
Mild, fruity

Color
Golden yellow

Alcohol Content
4.6%

ner on the market – combined, these products account for more than 80% of Mexico's total beer exports. To accommodate the demand for these beers and keep the beers fresh, Grupo Modelo owns eight breweries in Mexico, where all of their beer is brewed.

Calling All Parrot Heads

Corona's success can in part be attributed to marketing campaigns that, according to its web site, affiliate Corona with the best of Mexico. The campaigns don't just promote the beer, but "fun in the sun, warm hospitality, relaxation and good times."

A replica of a Corona delivery truck.

Advertising slogans include "Change Your Lattitude," inspired by song lyrics from the tropical-shirt wearing "parrot head" favorite Jimmy Buffett. Yet this isn't the only tie to Buffet. Corona has also been a sponsor of Buffet's concert tours for about the last 15 years, making its name nearly synonymous with his. The legions of "parrot heads" who attend Buffett's concerts no doubt enjoy their share of ice-cold Corona Extras!

Everyone loves Corona – even this inflatable parrot.

Corona Extra also sponsored Latin Grammy winner Luis Miguel's 2000 concert tour, as well as World Class Championship Boxing, the Indy Lights Races Series and Cart's Fed Ex Championship Series.

Corona's advertising campaign doesn't stray far from the successful fun-in-the-sun formula, either. It features Mexican beach scenes to further cement Corona as a beer brand for the

A Corona cooler is the coolest way to store your beer.

relaxed sun worshipper enjoying a tropical vacation, or for someone who just wants to reach that state of mind. According to a Barton Beer, Ltd. executive, in addition to its fun-and-sun image, Corona promotes a philosophy of not taking one's self too seriously. And advertising spots such as its 2000 Super Bowl commercial – featuring a lime flicked between two Corona bottles/goal posts on a beach – do just that.

Corona Extra's New Jacket

In the summer of 2000, Corona, which has always been known for its distinctive glass bottles with the blue-and-white painted labels, saw a different packaging for the beer. For the first time in the United States, Grupo Modelo introduced Corona in a can. The can is in the "wide mouth" style, which allows drinkers to add the lime wedge that is traditionally served with Corona. This introduction of can packaging was literally "just the ticket," as it allows Corona to be enjoyed in venues where glass bottles are restricted from being served, such as at arenas and stadiums.

Fun and sun in a can.

A Corona piñata.

Fun And Sun With Corona Extra

Corona Extra is a beer that is associated with fun times in the sunshine and the many products associated with the beer keep up that tradition. Click on *http://www.corona.com/securebuy.html* to learn more. Products without prices are available only at promotional events.

Baseball Jersey
$45.00

Beach Chair

Beach Ball

Golf Bag

Key Ring/Bottle Opener
$12.95

Bottle
Buddy

Travel Bag

Beach
Umbrella

T-Shirt

Go to CollectorsQuest.com for more
information on Corona Extra.

Corona Light

If you're thinking about enjoying a nice cold Corona Light on your next visit to your favorite Mexican vacation spot, you'd better think again. Corona Light, though brewed and bottled in Mexico, is only available in the United States. It was developed in response to the increasing popularity of, and demand for, light beers in the United States.

Corona Light coaster.

Corona Light made its way into the U.S. market in 1989, distinguishing itself as the first low-calorie Mexican beer. It caught on quickly, becoming to be the largest-selling Mexican light beer in the United States, selling over 1 million cases in its first year.

If you love the taste of Corona, but are counting your calories, you'll be glad to know that Corona Light has a low alcohol content. The two Coronas share other attributes as well. For example, although packaged to make it distinct from Corona Extra, Corona Light shares the older brand's fun-in-the-sun image. The two products are also often co-branded, which means that they share promotions and advertising.

A Member Of The Family

Other beers brewed by Grupo Modelo include Corona, Modelo Especial, Negra Modelo and Pacifico, all of which are carving out niches for themselves in the U.S. market.

In The Limelight

Lest anyone get the idea that Corona Light is simply riding on its more-established relative's coattails, it should be noted that Corona Light was given a "Hot Brand" award in 1997 by "Impact" magazine, an industry journal. To further establish Corona

Light as an independent brand, The Gambrinus Company, which imports Corona Light to the eastern United States, has in recent years stepped up its advertising for the brand, giving the beer its own slogans and identity. The "Miles Away From Other Light Beers" slogan of 1999, for example, is an attempt to drive home the fact that the beer is a "light." According to a Gambrinus executive quoted in "Beverage World," the Corona Light campaign " . . . presents Corona Light in the context of an alternative to other light beers, rather than as an alternative to Corona." Corona Light was portrayed as a flamingo in the ads, while other light beers were portrayed as buzzards.

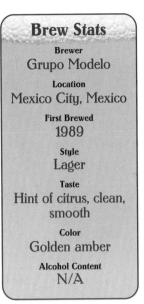

Brew Stats

Brewer
Grupo Modelo

Location
Mexico City, Mexico

First Brewed
1989

Style
Lager

Taste
Hint of citrus, clean, smooth

Color
Golden amber

Alcohol Content
N/A

Yo Quiero Corona Light

I want Corona! These products are giveaways at promotional events, but visit *http://www.corona.com/secure-buy.html* to find out what Corona Light fun-in-the-sun items you can buy.

Golf Bag

Hat

Swimsuit

Go to Collectors*Quest*.com for more information on Corona Light.

Dos Equis

What better way to practice all those years of Spanish classes than by ordering a beer? Dos Equis was first brewed in 1900, in a brewery called Cervecería Moctezuma, in Orizaba, Veracruz. The beer's original name was "Siglo XX," a name meant to signify the coming millennium. Eventually the name was changed to Dos Equis, but the "XX" logo remains, a familiar visual that instantly signifies the brand to its fans both in Mexico and around the world.

A Dos Equis coaster.

Although a Mexican beer, Dos Equis was first brewed by a German immigrant, Wilhelm Haase. Haase was a brewer by trade, and wanted to continue his profession in his new homeland of Mexico. He founded the Cervecería Moctezuma, and it was there that the Dos Equis tradition began.

Today, this amber lager is sold in more than 30 countries. Dos Equis holds the distinction of being the first Mexican beer to be served on draft in the United States. It also holds the honor of being a gold medal winner in the 1996 World Beer Cup.

What Do You Mean It's German Beer?

The brewer who developed Dos Equis was Wilhelm Haase, a German immigrant who came to Mexico in 1884.

In 1985, Cervecería Moctezuma was purchased by a parent company. It now operates under the Femsa Cerveza corporate umbrella. The brewing of Dos Equis takes place at breweries belonging to Cervecería Cuauhtémoc Moctezuma. Besides Dos Equis, this company produces **Bohemia, Carta**

Blanca, **Dos Equis Special Lager, Indio, Noche Buena, Sol, Superior, Tecate** and **Tecate Light** beer brands.

The United States of Dos Equis

Dos Equis is imported to the United States and marketed by Labatt USA. Advertisements for Dos Equis urge the prospective consumer to "Let your tastes travel," while promotions give away trips. If you're interested in traveling via advertising and the Internet, check out Dos Equis' web site at *http://www.femsa.com/beer/cart99/index.html* to view commercials that have aired all over the world.

Brew Stats

Brewer
Cervecería Moctezuma

Location
Orizaba, Veracruz, Mexico

First Brewed
1900

Style
Lager

Taste
Strong with balanced malt and hops

Color
Amber

Alcohol Content
4.7% (approx.)

X Marks The Treasure

There are plenty of ways to celebrate the millennium with these great Dos Equis products. X marks the spot for fun! Products without prices are promotional items.

Tap Handle

T-Shirt

Bottle Opener

Pint Glass
$4.50

Go to Collectors Quest.com for more information on Dos Equis.

Fat Tire Amber Ale

When you think of bicycling, you usually don't think of beer. Well, there was one person who made the connection. It was on a bicycle tour through Belgium that American Jeff Lebesch became so inspired by the local beer that he decided to

A look at the New Belgium Brewery.

start his own home-brew business. Teaming with his wife, Kim Jordan, Lebesch brewed, bottled and sold his new brew to local establishments during the early 1990s. In fact, Lebesch even worked as a delivery person for his venture.

Taking on the name the "New Belgium Brewing Company," Lebesch and Jordan's "suds"-sidiary has since grown to employ nearly 100 people, all of whom share a commitment to brewing a quality beverage and maintaining a clean environment. In fact, in 1998, New Belgium decided to purchase its power from an innovative source – the Fort Collins wind program.

Award-Winner

At the 2000 Great American Beer Festival, the New Belgium Brewing Company was named Mid-Size Brewing Company of the Year. Congratulations!

But life at New Belgium isn't just about conservation. Though they are known for their environmental and recycling efforts, the folks at New Belgium also like to have a good time. The company sponsors mountain bike tours and races (fitting, as this is how they got their start), including the "Ride The Rockies" annual bike tour, a fund raiser for local Colorado charities.

FAT TIRE
AMBER ALE

BOTTLED BY
NEW BEL   WING COMPANY, INC.
FORT COLLINS, COLORADO USA

Brews From New Belgium

The brewery's most popular ale is Fat Tire Amber Ale. Other beers the brewery produces are the Belgian monastery inspired **Abbey**, the high-alcohol content **Trippel** and a citrus-y **Sunshine Wheat**. Today, New Belgium brews are available in a select number of western states ranging from Washington to Missouri. New Belgium Brewery also offers a series of special-release beers that usually are offered for a limited time (approximately four month) and in a limited area (usually near the Colorado brewery). So if you're interested in any of these beers, it may be time to plan a trip (maybe even by bike!).

A Fat Tire bike race poster.

Brew Stats

Brewer
New Belgium Brewing Company, Inc.

Location
Fort Collins, Colorado

First Brewed
1991

Style
Ale

Taste
Malty

Color
Amber

Alcohol Content
5.3%

Fun With Fat Tire Amber Ale

The environmentally minded brewers from Colorado offer a plethora of products for you to purchase at *www.newbelgium.com* (the bottle opener is a promotional item).

— Bottle Opener

— T-Shirt
$17.00

Go to Collectors Quest .com for more information on Fat Tire Amber Ale.

Foster's Lager

Foster's Lager, known to Americans as "Australian for beer," is an internationally loved beer brand that is dedicated to bringing those of us not fortunate enough to live in the land "Down Under," a little bit of its culture.

Foster's – American For Beer?

This Foster's bottle opener looks just like a surfboard.

It may come as a surprise, then, to learn that Foster's was in fact the invention of two Irish Americans, the brothers W.M. and R.R. Foster. The Foster brothers came to Australia from New York City in 1886 and settled down in Melbourne with the goal of introducing a new kind of beer to the outback. And the Foster brothers were prepared: they brought with them state-of-the-art equipment, as well as an expert on the subject of refrigeration – Both of which would be imperative if their plan was to work. Soon after arriving in Melbourne, the brothers went about building the city's most modern brewery, which was specifically designed to brew their unique brand of bottom-fermented lager beer, a new concept for Australian beer drinkers.

Seeing Stars

Ever wondered what the stars on the Foster's label mean? The image represents a constellation called the Southern Cross, which is only visible from the S o u t h e r n Hemisphere, which is where Australia is located!

Before the introduction of the first Foster's in 1888, Australians were used to drinking traditional English ales, which are typically heavy and usually served warm. With this in mind, Foster's is made exactly the opposite: light and crisp, and best served cold.

FOSTER'S LAGER

12 Fl. Oz. = 355 mL

Will this boomerang-like coaster bring you more Foster's?

This, however, was not without its complications. You see, to brew and keep lager beer at the correct temperature requires refrigeration. So, with the help of the expert they had recruited, the Foster brothers built a 60-horsepower steam engine. This powered an ice-making machine, as well as a freezing apparatus that enabled cold brine to be pumped through six miles of pipe in order to cool the breweries' cellars and fermenting room. The beer was then stored in the racking room for 60 days at 35°F before being sent off for consumption by the Australian public.

Just keeping the beer cold for the fermenting process was not enough; once the beer was sent to the local pubs it had to be kept cold there as well – not an easy task in the days before electricity. The Foster brothers solved this problem by supplying those who stocked their beer with free ice daily. That ice came in handy, as Foster's was launched in the hot summer months, and its cold, refreshing taste made it an immediate success. In fact, in 1888, the same year Foster's was launched, it won the International Brewing Award at the Centennial Exhibition held in Melbourne. Surprisingly, despite this success, the Foster brothers sold their newly established company to a Melbourne syndicate and returned to America, leaving behind only the legacy of their name and the beer they had created.

Foster's Goes Global

Today, Foster's Lager is not just a local favorite, as it has grown into a worldwide phenomena. Besides Foster's Lager, other brands in the Carlton and United Breweries (CUB) family include **Victoria Bitter** (one of the most popular beers in Australia), **Foster's Light Ice**, **Carlton Cold** and **Crown Lager**. Worldwide, Foster's is

Brew Stats

Brewer
Carlton and United Breweries

Location
Melbourne, Australia

First Brewed
1888

Style
Lager

Taste
Malty, hoppy, crisp and clean

Color
Golden

Alcohol Content
4.9%

Courtesy of Dan Morean

A Foster's "oil" can.

brewed in nine countries and distributed to more than 135 countries. The global operations for Foster's are overseen by the international branch of the company, called, appropriately, Foster's International. To ensure that the quality and taste of Foster's Lager is universal, CUB employs its technical division, BrewTech, to make sure that each brewery lives up to its high standards.

Foster's says that it has an excellent drinkability and a full malt character that is balanced by a crisp, clean hop finish, which translates into light, tasty and refreshing. It is generally available on draft, and in all manner of bottles and cans, but the most interesting of the packaging possibilities is the Foster's "oil" can, a distinctive 26-ounce pop-top that resembles – you guessed it – an oil can.

How To Speak Australian

Foster's has become known for the fun and light-hearted advertisements that focus on what has become known as their beer's "Australianess." In fact, the company catalog features the tag line"Australian for Cool."

In the United States, Foster's is distributed by Molson USA, which also controls the marketing and sales of the beer in North America. Molson is responsible for the popular "How to Speak Australian" advertising campaign, which illustrates the adventuresome Australian attitude by giving larger-than-life items diminutive

GUPPY

A Foster's television advertisement.

names to show that Australians are not impressed by just anything. Since its introduction in 1994, the campaign has proved so popular that it has been translated into Spanish, French, German and even Mandarin!

Australian Acquisitions

There's no better way to show that you're a Foster's fan than by attiring yourself in their tees and hats. In fact, you don't have to stop there, check out their web site at *www.fostersbeer.com*.

Crop Top
$18.95

Golf Bag
$220.00

Hat
$5.50

Sweatshirt
$29.95

Varsity Jacket
$225.00

Polo Shirt
$17.95

T-Shirt
$3.95

Polo Shirt
$25.95

Go to CollectorsQuest.com for more information on Foster's Lager.

Genesee

Just as one might refer to a loved one with a special nickname, Genesee fans immediately say "Jenny" when asked the name of their favorite beer. Originally part of an ad campaign that ran from 1952 to 1963, the "ask for 'Jenny'" line can still be heard today not only in Genesee radio spots but

The Genesee Brewery in Rochester, New York.

also in bars serving the popular regional brew.

Founded by the Wehle family in Rochester, New York, in 1878, the Genesee Brewery distributes Genesee products to more than 30 states, as well to Canada. In addition to the original Genesee beer and a special seasonal beer called **Genesee Bock Beer**, several other brews are marketed under the Genesee name including **12 Horse Ale, Genny Cream Ale, Genny Ice, Genny Light, Genny Red** and the nonalcoholic **Genesee NA**. In ads for Genesee's 12 Horse Ale, its limited regional distribution is highlighted with the line "Hard to find. Easy to finish."

Genesee Brewing Company, which weighs in as the nation's fifth largest brewery, is instrumental in bringing a variety of beers to the marketplace. In fact, the company often works in the capacity of "contract brewer" (even producing one of Samuel Adams' beers).

Brew Stats

Brewer
Genesee Brewing Company

Location
Rochester, New York

First Brewed
1878

Style
Lager

Taste
Rich and strong

Color
Amber

Alcohol Content
5.0%

Looking To The Future

A Genesee coaster reflects the company's pride in its small size.

The beer industry has recently seen many breweries consolidate due to shrinking profits. As of this printing, the Genesee Brewing Company was in the process of changing from a family-owned and operated brewery to one owned by a private management company. According to Todd Brady, V.P. of Marketing and Development at Genesee, the deal should be finalized by the end of 2000.

Genesee On The Go

The following items are a taste of some of the different products available for purchase from Genesee's merchandise web page at *www.istonestreet.com.*

Genesee Sweatshirt $19.95

Genesee Hat $14.95

Genesee Jacket $59.95

Go to CollectorsQuest.com for more information on Genesee.

Grain Belt Premium

Grain Belt Premium took home the gold in 1994.

As its label proudly states, Grain Belt Premium is "the beer of exceptional quality" and has been since its debut in 1947. The history of the Grain Belt family of beers begins in 1893, when the very first bottle made its way from the production facility to the hands of a pub patron.

Grain Belt Premium has always stood out from the crowd. Its clear bottle gives beer afficionados a glimpse of the fine golden liquid that awaits within. But this is not the only tie-in between gold and grain belt: Grain Belt Premium took home the 1994 Great American Beer Festival gold medal for an American lager. While many beers have struggled to retain their popularity in an industry that sees breweries folding every day, Grain Belt Premium continues to exceed expectations, year-in, year-out.

Down In The Caves

The origins of the Minnesota Brewing Company date back to 1855, when Christopher Stahlmann established the Cave Brewery. He built the brewery along the banks of the Mississippi River in St. Paul, Minnesota, hoping to take advantage of the fresh spring water and excellent soil that would grow outstanding barley. The site was also home to underground caves – necessary for keeping beer cool before the advent of refrigeration.

Brew Stats

Brewer
Minnesota Brewing Company

Location
St. Paul, Minnesota

First Brewed
1947

Style
Lager

Taste
Crisp and refreshing

Color
Golden yellow

Alcohol Content
3.7%

The Cave Brewery exchanged hands many times after its initial sale in 1897. The Minnesota Brewing Company was the last outfit to purchase it, taking over in 1991. Despite its many brewers, however, the Grain Belt line has maintained its presence in the marketplace.

An artist's rendition of the Minnesota Brewing Company's early days.

Grain Belt's Cousins

In addition to Grain Belt Premium, **Golden Grain Belt** and **Golden Grain Belt Light** are also available to Grain Belt fans. The Minnesota Brewing Company has introduced other products to appeal to fans of craft beers. The **Brewer's Cave** line of beers (named after Stahlmann's caves) includes **Amber Wheat Ale, Black Barley Ale** and **Golden Caramel Lager**. The **Pig's Eye** line of beers (named after Pierre "Pig's Eye" Parrant, St. Paul's first settler) produces several beers including **Ice**, **Lean**, **N.A.**, **Pilsner** and **Red Amber**.

The Minnesota Brewing Company doesn't only produce alcohol products for drinking, however. They have diversified their interests into other areas and recently began manufacturing ethanol, an alternative fuel that is more friendly to the environment than gasoline or other fuels.

A Grain Belt label.

Getting The Grain Belt Goods

At the time of printing, the Minnesota Brewing Company was just starting up its on-line gift shop. Stop by *www.grainbelt.com* to see what they have to offer!

Go to Collectors*Quest*.com for more information on Grain Belt Premium.

Grolsch Premium Lager

In the historic Dutch town of Grolle on the banks of the river De Slinge, the Grolsch Brewery was founded almost 400 years ago. Although the brewery's history dates back to 1615, its first known owner was master brewer Peter Cuyper, who was appointed guild master of all the brewers in Grolle in 1677. It was Cuyper who perfected the natural method of brewing beer, a method that the Grolsch Brewery still uses to this day.

This Grolsch coaster takes on the look of a postcard.

Time has brought changes to Grolle. The town is now known as Groenlo, and the Grolsch Brewery has grown from a small, 17th-century operation to become the brewer of the best-selling premium beer in Holland, Grolsch Premium Lager. Grolsch has long been known for its unique swingtop bottle – a stopper bottle with a wire clamp – a design that has been used since 1897. The brewery commemorated the 100th anniversary of the swingtop bottles in 1997 with the release of six limited edition celebratory beers. The beers (Calixtus, De Vierde Wijze, De Twee Zwaluwen, Het Kanon, Lodewijk XIII and Picardijn) may very well prove to be collectors' items because of their limited production.

Brew Stats

Brewer
Grolsch Brewery

Location
Groenlo, Netherlands

First Brewed
1615

Style
Lager

Taste
Malty, strong-bodied

Color
Gold

Alcohol Content
5%

Besides Grolsch Premium Lager, which has been chosen three times as the "world's best beer" by the Beverage Testing Institute Inc. in the pale lager category, other members of the Grolsch family include **Grolsch Amber Ale** and **Grolsch Blond.**

A Time-Honored Tradition

Grolsch takes pride in its long history and loyalty to traditional brewing methods. This is evident in its advertising campaigns. In 1998, the company launched a series of radio commercials that tied the product in with its Dutch heritage and featured the tagline "Master Dutch brewers since 1615." A more recent billboard campaign inspired by the works of 17th-century Dutch painter Peter Paul Rubens, featured a barmaid with the words "Uplifting since 1615." The image of Grolsch's unique swingtop bottle is also used prominently in ads that promote the company's centuries-long family brewing heritage. Although more modern bottle designs are currently being marketed around the world, the traditional taste of Grolsch Premium Lager will remain.

A Grolsch coaster shows the renowned swingtop bottle.

Grolsch Goods

Want to get your hands on some of Grolsch's premium products? To find out what they have to offer, visit their official web site located at *www.grolsch.com.* Happy shopping!

Backpack
$38.50

Hat
$14.00

Polo Shirt
$24.50

Travel Bag
$72.00

Watch
$67.50

Go to CollectorsQuest.com for more information on Grolsch Premium Lager.

Guinness Stout

Question: Where do you go for the definitive answer to a trivia question and also to get the definitive Irish stout with a rich, creamy head? Answer: The Guinness Brewery in Dublin, Ireland!

A Guinness coaster contains a message of nostalgia.

Yes, the brewer of Ireland's arguably most famous beer is also the publisher of "The Guinness Book of World Records." The book was conceived in 1955 by the managing director of the Guinness Brewery to settle an argument at a party he was attending. This reference book (published with the brewery's backing) has since gone on to achieve worldwide success. The name Guinness, however, was already synonymous with what is arguably the most popular stout beer in the world.

Founded in 1759 when Arthur Guinness purchased an old brewery in Dublin, the Guinness Brewery first produced ale, a popular beer at the time. By the end of the century, however, another type of beer emerged. This beverage was popular among the porters who worked in London. This "porter" beer was exported from England to Ireland, and seriously affected sales of the local Irish beers.

A Record-Breaking Lease

Arthur Guinness signed a 9,000-year lease on an old, decrepit brewery on Dublin's St. James Street. By 1886, this brewery became the largest of its day. Today, it is one of the most modern breweries in the world.

As a result, Guinness formulated his own porter, which was made from roasted barley to give it its dark color. By 1799, Arthur Guinness brewed his last ale, and devoted his attentions entirely to the dark porter that is known today as Guinness Stout.

Variations On A Classic

Today, several types of Guinness Stout are on the market. Guinness Original, the modern version of the 18th-century porter, contains 4.3% alcohol by volume and is still brewed at the St. James Street brewery.

Guinness is also available in a four-pack format.

Guinness Draught was introduced in 1961 and is sometimes regarded as the definitive Guinness. It uses a mixture of carbon dioxide and nitrogen to deliver the signature Guinness rich, creamy head. It is said that if you draw a shamrock in the head of a freshly poured Guinness, the outline will remain until the last sip. Due to the invention of the "widget" – a device placed in cans to deliver the proper carbonation – Guinness Draught can also be served from a can without sacrificing flavor.

Guinness Foreign Extra Stout, a high-alcohol Guinness, was introduced when Guinness first began making shipments to overseas markets. The high-alcohol content helped the beer to survive long sea voyages. Today, overseas breweries produce this style of Guinness, and it is enjoyed in places such as Asia, Africa and the Caribbean.

Guinness is sold in more than 150 countries and brewed at 51 local breweries. Although Original Guinness, Guinness Draught and Guinness Foreign Extra Stout are the most predominant, there are about 20 different versions of Guinness worldwide.

Brew Stats

Brewer
Guinness Brewery

Location
Dublin, Ireland

First Brewed
1799

Style
Stout

Taste
Soft, creamy, dry

Color
Black

Alcohol Content
4.3%

Guinness Is Good For You

One of the most well-known slogans associated with Guinness is the phrase "Guinness is good for you." This early marketing pitch first appeared in the 1920s. Guinness had hired a marketing research firm to determine just what it was that people liked most about Guinness. The firm found that many people said that Guinness just made them feel good. Hence the slogan, with which many of today's Guinness drinkers would still agree.

A Guinness television advertisement depicts "the perfect pint."

Other popular campaigns from the early 20th century featured animal cartoons and the slogans "My goodness, my Guinness" and "Lovely day for a Guinness." Guinness continues its legacy of unique advertising today in campaigns such as the "Pour the perfect pint" and "Guinness refreshes the spirit" ads.

What really makes Guinness stand out, however, are its unique promotions and annual events, which are enjoyed by Guinness drinkers around the world. One such event that is held in pubs and bars across the United States is the annual "Great Guinness Toast" which takes place in February. At an appointed time, revelers raise a pint in a simultaneous toast, with the objective of breaking the world record for the "world's largest simultaneous toast." Perhaps the Great Guinness Toast most accurately represents the Guinness spirit – thousands united in celebration of this legendary brew, hoisting a pint of history.

Even ostriches enjoy Guinness, as this early 20th-century advertisement shows.

Toast With The most

The 2000 Great Guiness Toast had more than 320,000 toasters, a new world record. It will appear in the 2001 edition of "The Guiness Book of World Records," of course!

Bar Towel
$7.00

Get Your Guinness

Want to express your love of Guinness to the world? Now you can with the help of the shirts, towels, hats and other accessories available through the web site *www.pubshop.com*, which sells official Guinness merchandise.

T-Shirt
$20.00

Hat
$20.00

Pint Glass
$5.25

Shirt
$20.00

Go to Collectors*Quest*.com for more information on Guinness Stout.

111

Harp Lager

A noteworthy lager praised for its crisp, refreshing taste, Harp Lager is music to the ears of dedicated lager drinkers around the world. In 1959, when Guinness bought the Great Northern Brewery in Dundalk, Ireland, the brewery was renamed the Harp Lager Brewery and started producing the popular Harp Lager. The brew is now one of the fastest-growing import lagers in the United States.

This coaster displays the Harp logo.

A Lively Lager

Harp has been successfully marketed as being a cut above competing lagers. Early advertisements for the brand exclaimed "If it's just something cold and wet you want, drink water." Later slogans include "Harp stays sharp to the bottom of the glass" and "Common ground. Uncommon lager." Harp's high carbonation gives it quite a lively, effervescent appearance and this "liveliness" sets Harp apart from its competition.

The Celtic harp, from which the beer gets its name, appears on every Harp label (this traditional musical instrument is also the symbol for another Irish beer, Guinness). The origins of the harp are shrouded in mystery, dating back over a thousand years. According to

Brew Stats

Brewer
Harp Lager Brewery

Location
Dundalk, Ireland

First Brewed
1959

Style
Lager

Taste
Crisp, dry, bitter

Color
Golden

Alcohol Content
4.7% (approx.)

112

the legend that is printed on every Harp label, the image of the harp stands for quality and heritage.

Scrum Sponsors

The game of rugby dates back to the 1800s in Ireland abut has a much more recent history in the United States. Harp joined with USA Premier Rugby to form the Harp USA Rugby Super League for its inaugural 1996-97 rugby season. The Rugby Super League became the first rugby league in the United States and continues to grow in size and popularity.

Two Halves Equal Black And Tan

The "Black And Tan" or "Half And Half" is a combination of Harp Lager and Guinness Stout. When poured correctly, the tan Harp will go to the bottom of the glass, while the black Guinness will go to the top.

Play The Harp

Pay a visit to the on-line store What's On Tap at *www.pub-shop.com* to find these and other terrific Harp products for sale.

——— Hat
$20.00

——— Bar Towel
$7.00

Go to Collectors*Quest*.com for more information on Harp Lager.

Heineken

Everyone recognizes Heineken, with its familiar green bottle. But did you know that it was the first beer imported into the United States after the end of Prohibition in 1933? Heineken has been brewed in Holland since 1863, when Gerard Adriaan (G.A.)

The Heineken N.V. brewery in Amsterdam.

Heineken bought an Amsterdam brewery called The Haystack. It was the largest of the 69 breweries in the region and, with G.A. Heineken at the helm, demand for his beers grew quickly. In 1873, Heineken renamed the brewery after himself. Throughout the latter part of the 1800s, Heineken continued to experience growth and success, including winning the gold Medal of Honor at the World Exhibition in Paris.

Coming To America

By the early 1900s, under the leadership of Dr. Henry Pierre Heineken, G.A.'s son, the Heineken company was ready to conquer the United States. With the help of a Dutch immigrant named Leo van Munching (who would eventually become Heineken's the sole importer for the United States until 1991), Heineken got the word out about its product and was starting to see modest success in its new distribution area.

The High Price Of Success

In 1983, Freddy Heineken was kidnapped and held for three weeks until his family paid a ransom of $11.6 million. He was returned unharmed and the kidnappers were arrested and convicted.

114

A Heineken coaster.

By 1954, with G.A.'s grandson Alfred "Freddy" Heineken as chairman of the company, the Heineken name had gained such a sterling reputation that the decision was made to distribute Heineken beer to the rest of the world.

Dutch Treat

Heineken's sales and profit margins continued to grow throughout the latter half of the 20th century. The beer itself has changed very little and continues to be a dry, pilsner-style lager with a clean taste. Today, Heineken is consistently ranked among the top two imported beers in sales volume and has a growing portfolio of more than 80 regional and national brands. Additionally, Heineken N.V. produces two other international brands: **Amstel Light** and **Murphy's Irish Stout.**

Heineken has recently lost the distinction of being the world's second-largest brewer. They were recently defeated in a bidding war to acquire Bass PLC by Interbrew. With the acquisition of Bass, Interbrew has now gained the #2 spot. Heineken has no cause for concern, however, with sales remaining strong in more 170 countries that are located in more than five continents.

Brew Stats

Brewer
Heineken N.V.

Location
Amsterdam, Netherlands

First Brewed
1863

Style
Pilsner

Taste
Dry and clean

Color
Golden

Alcohol Content
4.9% (approx.)

A Tactful Tone

Prior to the 1970s, advertising was not a top priority for Heineken. Half-page black-and-white ads in publications like *The New Yorker* were common until the 1970s, when color ads began to showcase Heineken's distinctive green bottle. Television ads were straightforward and featured Heineken's status as "America's #1-selling imported beer." Ads on this same theme ran for 15 years with minimal changes.

In the late 1980s, however, Heineken changed tactics. Imported beer had suddenly become a hot item – but Heineken wanted their beer to be seen as something more than a trend. To that end, a 1988 ad campaign targeting trendy beers was launched featuring the tagline, "When you're done kidding around.

A Heineken six pack.

Heineken." By the beginning of the 1990s, Heineken was outselling its nearest competitor by more than two to one. For the next 10 years, Heineken relied on its reputation as the "best" to promote its beer that has been "true to the original recipe" for more than 125 years.

Humorous Heineken

Even Austin Powers teamed up with Heineken.

In 1999, Heineken chose to promote their beer with an ad that featured someone attempting to touch Mike Myers' "heinie" in a tie-in with the spy-spoof movie *Austin Powers: The Spy Who Shagged Me*. Heineken USA also produced a spot touting their status as a sponsor of the U.S. Open tennis tournament. In these commercials, ball boys and girls are crouched at various corners of a bar, poised to remove empty bottles of Heineken from tables, instead of tennis balls from the court.

In 2000, a series of ads made their debut that were dubbed "It's All About The Beer." One of the more popular ones was entitled "The Weasel" and featured a man who brings a six-pack of cheap beer to a party, only to stash it in the fridge and help himself to a highly superior bottle of Heineken.

The Weasel makes his move.

With its clever, topical ads, Heineken projects the image of sophistication and wit that it has been cultivating for more than 125 years.

T-Shirt

Key Chain

Key Chain

Hat

Chair

★ Heineken
US OPEN 2000

Shake Your "Heinie"

If Austin Powers has teamed up with
Heineken, the brew must be cool! Show
your coolness by scoring some of these
promotional items from a Heineken
retailer or bar event.

Go to CollectorsQuest.com for more
information on Heineken.

I.C. Light

With more than 130 years of experience brewing beer, it's no wonder that the Pittsburgh Brewing Company is as celebrated by Pittsburgh residents as other great Pittsburgh icons: the Pittsburgh Pirates, the Carnegie family and Andy Warhol. In fact, the

The Pittsburgh Brewing Company brewery.

Pittsburgh Brewing Company building enjoys wide recognition as a historic landmark and its different brands of beer are enjoyed by many of the city's residents.

The Right Choice Is The Light Choice

Because of its long history, Pittsburgh Brewing holds several distinctions. Its flagship **Iron City** brew is one of the first real lagers to be brewed in the United States (in 1861) and it is the first draught beer to be packaged in cans. It is also the first beer to come in commemorative cans honoring sporting teams, special events and historic sites.

When I.C. Light was introduced in 1978, the brand captured a hearty percentage of the light beer market and brought Pittsburgh Brewing national recognition. I.C. Light is low in carbohydrates as well as calories, which makes it perfect for beer drinkers who wish to stick to their low-carb diets. **I.C. Light Twist** is a seasonal variation of I.C. Light and features a hint of lime.

Brew Stats

Brewer
Pittsburgh Brewing Company

Location
Pittsburgh, Pennsylvania

First Brewed
1976

Style
Lager

Taste
Smooth and bitter

Color
Light yellow

Alcohol Content
3.3%

A specialty I.C. Light can.

I.C. Light can be purchased in nearly 30 states from coast to coast. But I.C Light and Iron City are not the only brands in the Pittsburgh Brewing family. One of their other brands, which is available in a more limited region, is **Augustiner Lager,** named after Augustiner, Germany, home of the famous annual Oktoberfest festival.

Pittsburgh Brewing In The Iron City

I.C. Light and its big brother, Iron City, show their Pittsburgh pride by wearing the black and gold colors of the city, colors shared by Pittsburgh's sports teams the Penguins, Steelers and Pirates.

Perhaps the most significant method of advertising for the regional brewery is through sponsoring local events. The brewery hosts an annual Oktoberfest of their own that features German food, musical entertainment and of course – beer! Other events include the I.C. Light Waiter Waitress Cup and a Halloween Boo & Brew.

Black And Gold Pride

Show your love for the black and gold of I.C. Light by using these products from the Pittsburgh Brewing Company. Go to *www.pittsburgh-brewingco.com/store* to learn more (the key chain is a promotional item).

T-Shirt
$10.00

Key Chain

Go to CollectorsQuest.com for more information on I.C. Light.

Labatt Blue

Since 1951, Canadians and Americans alike have enjoyed a "a case of the blues," for this was the year that Labatt Blue made its debut. Since then, the award-winning brew

Inside the Labatt brewery in Canada

has made quite a name for itself – it is the #1 beer in Canada and the #3 import in the United States.

The Labatt Brewing Company has been producing quality beer for more than 150 years. The company was founded in 1847 by John Kinder Labatt, the company has become a leader in the brewing industry. Labatt's flagship brand, Labatt Blue, was originally introduced as Labatt Pilsner. The beer eventually earned the name "blue" because of its label's color and Labatt's association with the Winnipeg football team, the Blue Bombers.

Kidnapped!

In 1934, John S. Labatt was kidnapped by gangsters in London, Ontario, Canada. He was released a week later in Toronto. As a result of this extremely traumatic experience, Labatt became very reclusive.

A Company Of Firsts

Labatt was responsible for many Canadian firsts in the world of beer including the twist top, light beer, non-alcoholic beer and light ale. Even more impressive is they made the world's first Ice Brewed™ beer.

Meet The Family

In Canada today, there are eight Labatt breweries located in five regions. Other beers produced by Labatt include **Labatt Blue Light, Labatt ICE, Labatt Wildcat** and **Kokanee.** Labatt is also

Brew Stats

Brewer
Labatt Brewing Company

Location
London, Ontario Canada

First Brewed
1951

Style
Pilsner

Taste
Fruity character, light and crisp

Color
Golden

Alcohol Content
5.0%

licensed to brew Guinness Extra Stout and Budweiser for the Canadian market.

Advertising

In 1999, Labatt Blue launched its first U.S. television advertising campaign. This series of four humorous spots features a man in a bear suit and the tagline "Labatt Blue: pure Canada." Viewers follow the "bear" on a bus trip from Canada to New York, then see him try to purchase beer, dine at a sushi bar and sing karaoke, get spray painted by fur protesters and take a ride with a beautiful woman.

The "bear" has had many adventures.

Shopping Cures The Blues

You can get these products from *www.labattblue.com.* Availability of items can vary from season to season.

Muskoka Chair

Roots Jacket

Hockey Jersey

Hockey Bag

Go to CollectorsQuest.com for more information on Labatt Blue.

Leinenkugel's Original Lager

Any way you pronounce it,
Leinenkugel is a mouthful.

In some ways, Chippewa Falls, Wisconsin, is like many other towns that dot the northern United States. But what put Chippewa Falls on the map was beer. The secret is out about the Jacob Leinenkugel Brewing Company's luscious lagers and Chippewa Falls has become a a popular destination for tourists on beer pilgrimages.

Established by Jacob Leinenkugel in 1867, the Jacob Leinenkugel Brewing Company supplied beer to thirsty loggers after a hard day at the mills. After Jacob's death in 1899, the company was presided over by his son Matt, establishing a family-run tradition that continues today. Even after "Leinie's," as the small company is nicknamed, was bought by industry giant Miller Brewing Company in 1988, it remained a family business. In 1989, the brewery welcomed a fifth-generation Leinenkugel to the top spot within the company.

First brewed in 1867, Leinenkugel's Original Lager is as old as the brewery itself. Its medley of multiple malts creates a distinct flavor that was an award winner at the 1987 Great American Beer Festival in the category of best American premium light lager. Leinenkugel also produces several other beers including **Leinie's Light, Creamy Dark, Honey Weiss, Northwoods, Red,** tap-exclusive **Hefeweizen** and the seasonals **Berry Weiss** and **Bock.**

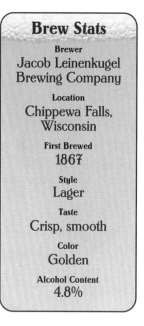

Brew Stats

Brewer
Jacob Leinenkugel
Brewing Company

Location
Chippewa Falls,
Wisconsin

First Brewed
1867

Style
Lager

Taste
Crisp, smooth

Color
Golden

Alcohol Content
4.8%

Courtesy of Dan Morean

A Leinenkugel cone top can.

Several memorable promotions have grabbed the attention of shoppers. The Leinie Lodge Tackle Box was a holiday gift pack that included a selection of 12 Leinenkugel beers in a tackle box–shaped package. The company's Fan Pack pleased Green Bay Packer fans who could wear the cheese wedge–shaped carton as a hat once they polished off the 15 cans of Honey Weiss it contained.

As Leinie's popularity has grown, the company has branched out into new locations. In 1995, Leinenkugel set up shop in Milwaukee's defunct Tenth Street Brewery. Since few things beat a cold beer at a baseball game, Leinie's scored a home run when it introduced Leinenkugel's Ballyard Brewery outside Bank One Ballpark in Phoenix, Arizona, home of the Arizona Diamondbacks baseball team.

Line Up For Leinenkugel

Check with your Leinenkugel retailer to find out how you can buy these great items.

Gym Bag

Hat

T-Shirt

Water Bottle

Go to CollectorsQuest.com for more information on Leinkenkugel's Original Lager.

Magic Hat #9

What the heck does Magic Hat #9 mean? You're out of luck, because according to the brewers at Vermont's Magic Hat Brewing Company, the meaning of the name will *never* be revealed! Magic Hat #9, the beer "cloaked in

The Magic Hat brewery in Vermont.

secrecy" and brewed "clandestinely," is one of the many magical concoctions from this brewery that specializes in beers with names like **Hocus Pocus**, a beer made of "equal parts delirium and divine intervention" and **Heart Of Darkness,** a stout "filled with the howling of black dogs . . .".

Elixir Of Life

The success of the Magic Hat Brewery is a result of diligence, hard work and, maybe, just a little bit of magic conjured forth by founders Alan Newman and Bob Johnson. Their first brewing attempt, christened Magic Hat Ale, was originally bottled in November, 1994, by The Shipyard Brewing Company, a microbrewery located in Portland, Maine. Renamed **Bob's First Ale,** this Irish-style red ale became Magic Hat's flagship ale when the brewery opened in 1995.

Magic Hats!

As proponents of safe sex, the owners of Magic Hat provide educational information regarding the prevention of AIDS on their web site *www.magichat.net.*

#9 Is The Charm

With the taste of success on their lips, Newman and Johnson decided to expand their repertoire. Magic Hat #9 was originally brewed as a "seasonal teaser" but its popularity forced the brewery to continue offering the tasty ale with the psychedelic label on

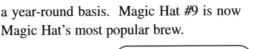
a year-round basis. Magic Hat #9 is now Magic Hat's most popular brew.

Finding Magic Hat brews is easy – if you live in New England or in Maryland, thanks to a beer distributor who tasted Magic Hat at a holiday party in Vermont and decided to carry the magic back to his home state of Maryland. Known for the imaginative names and label designs for its beers, Magic Hat also offers **Humble Patience**, **Blind Faith** and **Fat Angel** and, depending upon the time of year, you can also enjoy **Miss Bliss** and **Jinx**. Occasionally, other brews are released, depending upon "when the spirits move" them!

A Magic Hat Brewing Company coaster.

Brew Stats

Brewer
Magic Hat Brewing Company

Location
South Burlington, Vermont

First Brewed
1995

Style
Pale ale

Taste
Dry, crisp, and fruity

Color
Yellow Gold

Alcohol Content
5.1%

The Magic Of Magic Hat #9

These items are available for purchase at either the Magic Hat Brewery or at their web site at *www.magichat.net.*

T-Shirt
$16.00

Pint Glass
$13.00/set of four

Hat
$18.00

Bottle Opener
$5.00

Go to Collectors Quest.com for more information on Magic Hat #9.

Michelob

From its gold foil-wrapped brown glass to its contoured curves, a bottle of Michelob exists in a class of its own. Although Michelob is now known for its distinctive bottle, it's surprising to learn that Michelob was not available in bottles for more than 50 years after its introduction.

An Anheuser-Busch brewery.

An Anheuser-Busch Exclusive

This super-premium beer was originally available only on draft. Michelob remained a draft exclusive until 1961, when it first became available in bottles. Just five years later, Michelob was sold in cans, making a high-class product available in a six-pack format.

The secret behind Michelob's smooth taste lies in the malt. Imported hops and two-row barley give the beer its smooth flavor and full body.

Superior quality light beer became a reality in 1978 when **Michelob Light** was introduced, becoming the first super-premium light beer in the United States. History was made again in 1988, with the introduction of **Michelob Dry**. The Michelob family also includes **Michelob Golden Draft**, **Michelob Amber Bock**, **Michelob HefeWeizen**, **Michelob Honey Lager** and **Michelob Black & Tan**.

Brew Stats

Brewer
Anheuser-Busch

Location
St. Louis, Missouri

First Brewed
1896

Style
Lager

Taste
Smooth, sweet

Color
Pale, golden

Alcohol Content
5.0%

Michelob – "America's Beer"?

Anheuser-Busch has always marketed Michelob as an upscale beer. Early advertisements portrayed well-to-do socialites exclaiming "I don't care what it costs . . . I want it!" when discussing Michelob. The slightly wordy slogan "In beer, going first class is Michelob. Period." was replaced by the popular "Weekends were made for Michelob" campaign. More recent slogans include "The night belongs to Michelob," "Some days are better than others" and "Beer or Michelob?"

A Michelob television advertisement asks a good question.

Michelob is also at home on golf courts, tennis courts and polo fields across the world. Team Michelob Light enjoys the status of being considered "America's Team" in the competitive world of championship polo.

America's Beer Gear

These clothing items are just a point-and-click away from being yours at *www.budshop.com*.

Polo Shirt
$37.00

Hat
$10.00

T-Shirt
$9.00

Go to CollectorsQuest.com for more information on Michelob.

Miller Genuine Draft

How did you choose your favorite beer? Or are you still searching for it? Just take a stroll down the aisles of your favorite beer retailer – there are so many beers to choose from! One of the brewing companies to thank for the wide selection of beer is the Miller Brewing Company of Milwaukee,

The Plank Road Brewery in Milwaukee, Wisconsin.

Wisconsin, who currently produces over *sixty* different brands of beer! Out of those, however, three brands stand out – **Miller High Life**, **Miller Lite** and Miller Genuine Draft, the company's current top sellers.

The Colder, The Better

Miller Genuine Draft first appeared on American shelves in 1985 as "Miller High Life Genuine Draft." This new brand was brewed using "a unique cold filtration process" called ceramic cold filtration, in which beer is forced through a special ceramic filter in order to remove microscopic impurities.

Cold filtration was used as an alternative to the heat-pasteurization method used by other beer manufacturers and, in addition to granting shelf stability to the beer, it also allowed the brew to retain the smoothness of a draft beer without requiring constant refrigeration.

Spelunking

Years before artificial refrigeration was invented, a series of caves located deep underground on the Miller Brewery property was used to keep beer barrels cold. These caves are open for touring – stop in for a visit!

The Genuine Article

After experiencing success in selected test markets, Miller High Life Genuine Draft became available throughout the continental United States by mid-1986. The name of the beer was shortened to Miller Genuine Draft (MGD) and, in 1991, its popularity inspired a light version, **Miller Genuine Draft Light**.

A Miller Genuine Draft coaster promotes a travel contest.

This coaster reinforces the "Miller time" philosophy.

With MGD packaged in clear bottles, it is easy to see that "it's Miller time!" And, now, with the widespread availability of Miller Genuine Draft in clear *plastic* bottles – which are resealable, recyclable and unbreakable – "America's Genuine Draft" is the perfect brew to include in your picnic basket at the beach, in the cooler at the pool or in your hand at your favorite sports arena.

For the past four years, Miller Genuine Draft has received silver and gold medals in various categories at the Great American Beer Festival held annually in Boulder, Colorado. International sales of Miller Genuine Draft have gradually increased, and it is currently brewed in eight countries (Canada, Brazil, Great Britain, Ireland, Jordan, the Philippines, Japan and Russia). Russia recently signed a licensing agreement to start brewing it locally.

Big Bikes, Big Beer . . .

With their corporate headquarters literally blocks apart in downtown Milwaukee, Miller Brewing Company and Harley-

Brew Stats

Brewer
Miller Brewing Company

Location
Milwaukee, Wisconsin

First Brewed
1985

Style
Lager

Taste
Smooth, light, hearty

Color
Golden

Alcohol Content
5.0%

Davidson, Inc. have been teaming up for promotional and commercial ventures for a number of years. In 1993 and 1998, Miller Genuine Draft sponsored the anniversary reunions for Harley-Davidson's 90th and 95th years in business. In a Miller Brewing promotion, more than 50 Harley-Davidson motorcycles were given away in conjunction with the 1998 reunion.

The collaboration continued in 1999 when Harley-Davidson and Miller held another motorcycle sweepstakes in conjunction with the promotion "Instant Summer, Just Add Beer." Spectators at NASCAR races have also seen the new Miller/Harley-Davidson navy-blue-and-chrome designs featured on the cars driven by the Miller-sponsored race teams of Rusty Wallace, Max Papis and Larry Dixon.

. . . And Blind Dates

For the past three years, Miller Genuine Draft has sponsored the MGD Blind Date concert tour, which has featured top acts like the Red Hot Chili Peppers, Foo Fighters, Hole and Beck. Lucky contest winners receive tickets for these concerts held at small venues in Las Vegas, Chicago, Philadelphia, San Francisco, Los Angeles and Dublin, Ireland – and transportation to the show is also included! Just

like any blind date, the identity of the concert performers is kept a secret until the minute the curtain rises at the beginning of the shows.

In addition to these popular promotional events, the Miller Brewing Company has released several memorable television commercials. A recent campaign focuses on Miller Genuine Draft's untainted flavor. The message of the ads is that even though the beer is packaged in bottles, it has the same great taste as beer that is tapped from a fresh keg. In effect, the bottles are nothing but mini-kegs, and "every cap is a tap."

These Miller Genuine Draft TV advertisements promote its keg-in-a-bottle taste.

Miller Genuine Merchandise

Ask your Miller Genuine Draft retailer how to purchase this array of products, as well as much more.

CD Case

Hat

Golf Bag

Tank Top

Go to CollectorsQuest.com for more information on Miller Genuine Draft.

Miller High Life

Miller High Life is the oldest of the beers in the Miller family, with a lineage dating back to the company's beginnings in 1855. Back then it was known as plain Miller Beer, and continued to be sold under that name throughout the 19th century.

An early Miller High Life delivery wagon.

As the 20th century dawned, however, the company decided that it wanted its flagship brand to have a more distinctive name. Carl Miller, company president at the time, sent his uncle Ernst to scour the country in search of a suitable name. Nothing struck Ernst's fancy until he got to New Orleans, and noticed a factory producing High Life cigars. The Miller Brewing Company bought out the factory, and in 1904 Miller High Life went on sale for the first time. Two years later, the "champagne of bottle beer" slogan was first used. This brand's signature clear bottle also compliments the slogan, showcasing the grand color of the beer (and also helps bartenders see when customers need another beer).

When the Philip Morris conglomerate bought out the Miller family in 1970, they shortened the slogan to "champagne of beers" and decided to change High Life's image. A new advertising campaign declared it's "Miller time." It certainly was Miller's time, as between 1970 and 1980, sales of the brand increased fourfold. Then, the brand reached its high-water mark in 1981, with annual sales of 23 million barrels.

Birth Of The High Life

What a deal! For $25,000, the Miller Brewing Company bought the High Life name, which first belonged to a cigar maker. For their money, the brewery got the name, the factory and everything inside it.

Image Is Everything

A Miller High Life coaster.

Bruce Winterton, a brand manager for Miller Brewing, considers Miller High Life a pioneer in image marketing. "Miller High Life was the first to push image as part of the brand promotion in the '70s, with 'Miller Time,'" she says. Miller was also among the first brands to go on national sports programming and push image.

In 1985, Miller High Life tried to capitalize on Bruce Springsteen's "Born In The U.S.A." image with their claim, "Miller's made the American way, born and brewed in the U.S.A." In 1998, Miller decided to give High Life another advertising push, with a series of commercial spots re-emphasizing High Life's blue-collar appeal. Sales of the brand have been increasing since then, and though High Life has not regained its status as Miller's top seller, it does hold a spot in the company's Big Three.

A Miller High Life beer tray.

In 1998, Miller ads worked to reinforce the image of Miller High Life as a "working man's beer" through a series of amusing commercials. In one very memorable commercial, titled "Duct Tape," a man uses good-for-everything duct tape to repair a broken refrigerator handle while a voice-over deadpans, "the High Life man knows that if the pharaohs had duct tape, the Sphinx would still have a nose. We salute you, duct tape. You help a man get to Miller Time."

In 1989, almost 10 years before, the High Life advertisements centered around the

Brew Stats

Brewer
Miller Brewing Co.

Location
Milwaukee, Wisconsin

First Brewed
1904

Style
Lager

Taste
Sweet, smooth

Color
Golden

Alcohol Content
N/A

A recent Miller High Life print ad encourages you to satisfy your card-playing buddies.

For Every Man

The "Miller Time" slogan was developed to attract blue-collar drinkers to High Life because the "champagne of bottle beer," slogan made it appear to be a rich man's beer.

theme "the best comes shining through," and showed everyday Americans doing good deeds – from a group of farmers harvesting the crops of a recently widowed neighbor to a race-car driver alerting his competitor to a potentially fatal flaw in his car. How do you reward such good deeds? The commercials had another tagline to answer that question: "Buy that man a Miller."

A more recent ad campaign is aimed at men who have poker nights with their buddies. It depicts a shopping trip, encouraging the host to fill up his cart and his guests' bellies with good food. While some may argue that the several raw pounds of meat pictured in the ad may not be the tastiest of sights, no one will argue that plenty of Miller High Life is more than appealing. The point of the ad: a gastronomically satisfied man will more easily part with his money. After all, we have all heard that the way to a man's heart is through his stomach.

Live The High Life

The next time you go to buy your favorite beer, ask the retailer how you can make Miller High Life products a part of your life.

Beach Ball

Lamp

Sweatshirt

Hat

Fold-Up Chair

Go to CollectorsQuest.com for more information on Miller High Life.

Miller High Life

Miller Lite

Miller Lite was not the first light beer sold in America, but it was the first one to find widespread success. While other light beers had been marketed as early on as the 1960s, it took the magic of Miller to show the world the appeal of this great-tasting innovation.

"Cap off" your day with a Miller Lite.

Miller Lite was born when the Miller Brewing Company bought out the brewery that produced Meister Bräu. Among its products, Meister Bräu had sold a brand called Meister Bräu Lite, which had seen minimal success among beer-drinkers. Miller tinkered with the recipe, re-packaged the brew and renamed it Miller Lite. Test-marketed in 1973 and introduced nationally in 1975, Miller Lite enjoyed far more success than Meister Bräu Lite. In fact, its success surprised every-one as sales of Miller Lite soon skyrocketed past those of **Miller Genuine Draft** and **Miller High Life**.

Like Miller Genuine Draft, Miller Lite was so successful that it had an offshoot of its own: **Miller Lite Ice**, the first low-calorie ice beer, introduced in 1994. Miller Lite Ice was basically Miller Lite that was reduced to subfreezing temperatures during the brewing process. When the ice crystals that formed in the beer were removed, they resulted in a smoother, richer-tasting beer that also had a higher alcohol content. Miller Lite Ice appeared at a time when ice beers were a new innovation,

Miller Lite All-Stars

The roster of famous celebrities appearing in Miller Lite's "Tastes Great-Less Filling" commercials includes Dick Butkus, Lee Meredith, Bob Uecker, Bubba Smith, and Mickey Spillane.

A Miller Lite neon sign.

and the company continues to brew it today. In addition to Miller Lite and Miler Lite Ice, the Miller Brewing Company is responsible for a wide variety of other premium, light and ice beer brands which include the familiar **ICEHOUSE**, **Sharp's**, **Shipyard** and **Red Dog**.

Why was Miller Lite so successful when other light beers had failed? Miller Lite is brewed with the highest-quality ingredients and the utmost care, so as to cut back on the calories without sacrificing great taste. The brand was also boosted by a highly successful ad campaign.

The Great Debate

Rather than advertise the beer as a "diet drink," like other breweries had done with their light beers, Miller released a series of commercials centered around the slogan "everything you always wanted in a beer – and less" to introduce the beer to the American public. The commercials featured ex-athletes and other recognizable stars (including comedian Rodney Dangerfield) debating the merits of Miller Lite: was it a great beer because it tasted so good, or because it didn't fill you up? The "everything . . . and less" campaign featured the tagline "tastes great, less filling," a reference to the athletes' barroom debates.

Brew Stats

Brewer
Miller Brewing Company

Location
Milwaukee, Wisconsin

First Brewed
1973

Style
Lager

Taste
Mild and refreshing with high bitterness

Color
Golden

Alcohol Content
4.6%

Taking this approach helped Miller to keep Miller Lite targeted at the beer-drinking audience rather than the calorie-conscious crowd. The light hearted commercials, which kept viewers anticipating who would be the next familiar face to wander into the Miller bar, were among the most popular of their time.

Miller In The Ring

The "tastes great, less filling" campaign took a new spin in a memorable series of spots in the summer of 1989. Dubbed "Lite-a-mania," the ads were billed as an attempt to settle the "tastes great-less filling" debate through a pro-wrestling parody, with wrestler (and at that time future governor) Jesse Ventura representing "tastes great," fighting a mysterious "Masked Marauder" who personifies "Less Filling." After nine weeks the promotion ended with the news that Tastes Great won, after Ventura decked the Marauder and unmasked him, revealing baseball personality Bob Uecker, a Lite pitchman. Ventura was also unmasked to reveal another Lite pitchman, football player L.C. Greenwood. Finally, announcer Vince McMahon was unmasked, and turned out to be Sonny Bono, the former singer and then mayor of Palm Springs, California.

Smell My Beer!

In 1998, Miller Lite cans were issued with "scratch and sniff" stickers that contained scents associated with those of summer – including pizza, beef and coconut. Each scent corresponded with a prize.

Calling All Sports Fans

A six-pack of Miller Lite.

Since then, Miller Lite has made its way into the realms of football, baseball, auto racing and boxing through a variety of promotions, advertisements and sponsorships. Miller Park is in the process of being built to replace baseball's Milwaukee County Stadium and will soon house the Milwaukee Brewers. A sweepstakes program has run for the past few years that sends a lucky winner to the Super Bowl each year. And Miller Lite has been a sponsor for NASCAR driver Rusty Wallace for several years.

A recent advertising campaign for Miller Lite featured a hospitalized man with a steel plate in his head. His roommates, having heard that he gets radio reception through the plate, turn the man's head from side to side until they find a broadcast of the big "game."

Who knew that a steel plate in your head could allow you to tune in a radio station!

Miller's advertising is mainly targeted at men, as is evident by another recent advertisement featuring supermodel Rebecca Romjin-Stamos. Romjin-Stamos appears in a print ad for the company that reads "Pilsner is a type of beer. Kind of like Rebecca is a type of woman."

The company has also recently released advertising that features the merits of responsible drinking. Miller Brewing Company has always prided itself on promoting awareness of responsible drinking and takes that effort a step further with a new television spot that features a sober man leaving his drunken friends behind so he can drive three beautiful women home. The spot brings back the tagline "it's Miller time," which has become associated over the years with good times and good friendship.

A provocative Miller Lite print ad.

Sweatshirt

Umbrella

Lava Lamp

Dress

Hammock

Let This Lite Lead The Way

Your Miller Lite retailer can help you purchase a wide array of products, some of which you see here.

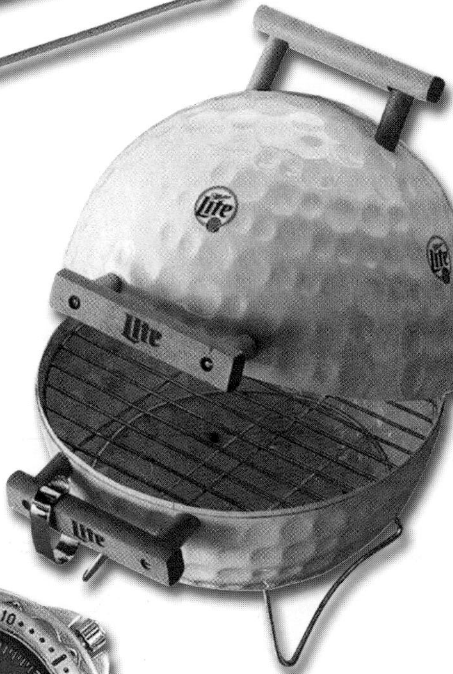

Golf Ball Grill

Watch

Go to CollectorsQuest.com for more information on Miller Lite.

Milwaukee's Best

Affectionately referred to as the "Beast" by its fans, Milwaukee's Best offers great taste at an affordable price. According to the 2000 *Adams Beer Handbook*, it was ranked as the #12 top-selling beer in 1999, perhaps

A look where Milwaukee's Best is brewed by the Miller Brewing Company in Milwaukee.

partly due to new packaging and an advertising campaign that encouraged beer drinkers across the country to "unleash the beast."

Milwaukee is often called the "beer capital of the world," so it's no surprise to anyone that this best-selling beer hails from that great beer-making city. In fact, Milwaukee's Best was also one of Milwaukee's first, as the A. Gettelman Brewing Company started brewing the beer about 50 years after the city established its charter in 1846.

Fun Facts

In 1892, A. Gettelman Brewing introduced a "Hospital Tonic" that was acclaimed by local doctors. It was commonly used by nursing mothers until it went out of production.

Gettelman Gets It Started

The A. Gettelman Brewing Company was founded in 1854 in Milwaukee by George Schweickhart, and it was originally known as the Menominee Brewery. George's son-in-law, Adam Gettelman, took over the reins of the company in 1876 and it is for him that the company was named. Gettelman produced several popular beers including Stein Brew,

142

An old-style
Milwaukee's Best can.

Milwaukee's Best and $1,000 Beer, which was famous for its claim that $1,000 would be given to anyone who could prove that anything besides pure malt and hops had been used in the beer. No one ever collected the money.

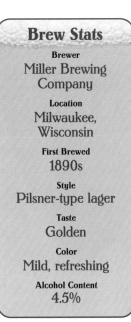

Brew Stats

Brewer
Miller Brewing Company

Location
Milwaukee, Wisconsin

First Brewed
1890s

Style
Pilsner-type lager

Taste
Golden

Color
Mild, refreshing

Alcohol Content
4.5%

As the A. Gettelman Brewing Company continued to prosper, it was passed down through generations of Gettelmans until January 14, 1961, when the Miller Brewing Company expanded their holdings by purchasing Gettelman. Miller continued to produce the Gettelman brands until the mid-1970s when they were all discontinued to provide more room for the more popular products – Miller Lite and Miller High Life. Miller reintroduced Milwaukee's Best in 1984.

The Miller Family Tree

Two additions have been made to the Milwaukee's Best family. **Milwaukee's Best Light**, which ranked as the #16 beer in 1999, was introduced in 1986 and **Milwaukee's Best Ice** was a more recent introduction, in 1994. Miller now produces and imports over 60 different beers and operates six separate brewing facilities. Other Miller brands include **ICEHOUSE**, **Sharp's** and **Red Dog**.

The Miller family of beers.

Go to Collectors*Quest*.com for more information on Milwaukee's Best.

Modelo Especial

Next time you visit a Mexican restaurant, you may want to think twice before ordering your usual Mexican beer. There is a wide variety of Mexican beers available in the United States that are crisp and refreshing and taste great with everything from tacos to tamales (and American fare, as well).

Modelo Especial cans in a six-pack.

Modelo Especial is brewed by Grupo Modelo (the brewery that also produces Corona Extra and Corona Light). The company, which was founded in 1925 as Cervecería Modelo, S.A., is the #1 producer of beer in Mexico. In addition to five brands that are available exclusively in Mexico, Grupo Modelo exports five beers to the United States, including **Corona Extra**, **Corona Light**, **Negra Modelo**, **Pacifico Clara** and of course, Modelo Especial.

The #1-selling canned beer in Mexico, Modelo Especial crossed the border into the United States in 1985 in canned form, and first became available in bottled six-packs in 1990. While it has yet to reach #1 status in the United States, Modelo Especial consistently ranks in the top-15 on import lists and is gaining in popularity Hispanic communities, as well as in the general population.

Making An Impact

Modelo Especial has been named a "hot brand" by *Impact* magazine, reflecting its growth and above-average performance in the beer market.

Fans of lighter lager beers can't go wrong with this Mexican brew. It's said to have a little more flavor than most domestic lagers, and is crisp and refreshing. Modelo Especial is medium bodied and goes down smooth, especially with spicy Tex-Mex or Mexican dishes.

So next time you have a hankering for a cold brew and want to have a little South of the Border fun, try a Modelo Especial – you won't be disappointed.

Modelo For The Masses

Modelo merchandise is available through a number of different outlets. See your local retailer for more information on how to obtain T-shirts, key chains and more.

Brew Stats

Brewer
Grupo Modelo

Location
Mexico City, Mexico

First Brewed
1966

Style
Pilsner

Taste
Well balanced, medium bodied

Color
Pale amber

Alcohol Content
N/A

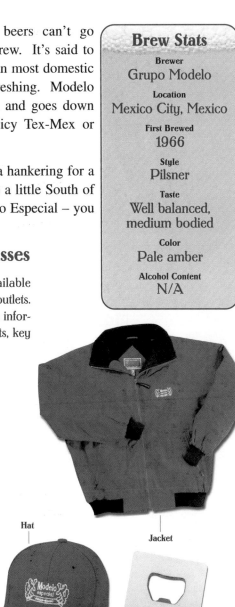

Golf Bag

Hat

Jacket

Modelo especial — Bottle Opener

Go to CollectorsQuest.com for more information on Modelo Especial.

Molson Canadian

Many things come to mind when you first see a Molson Canadian bottle. Its distinctive bright-red maple leaf makes it hard not to think of Canada. And the Molson name often brings hockey to mind, as the company has been closely associated with the sport since 1957. Molson

Outside the Molson Brewery in Montreal.

also has sponsored Indy car racing in Toronto and Vancouver. And whether you prefer watching action on the ice or on the racetrack, there is no doubt that a smooth, refreshing Molson Canadian makes the perfect game-day brew.

More Than 200 Years Of Beer

The Molson family's association with beer dates all the way back to 1786, when at the young age of 22, John Molson Sr. left his native country of England and became sole proprietor of his own brewery near Montreal. Molson brewed more than 4,000 gallons that first year and two years later more than tripled that output. Molson's success continued until 1836, the company's 50th anniversary, when it mourned the death of its founder, John Molson Sr. Luckily, his family was ready to take up the reins and continue the business, and by the company's 100th anniversary there had been a 175-fold increase in volume. By 1936 – the company's 150th anniversary – almost 7 million gallons were being produced.

Rinkside Brew

In 1999, Molson opened a small brewery in Toronto's Air Canada Centre (home of the Maple Leafs and Raptors). Two exclusive specialty beers have been created for this location.

146

The 1950s and 1960s saw Molson begin an era of expansion. Several new breweries were purchased and new brands were released – **Molson Golden** in 1954, **Crown and Anchor** (their first lager) in 1955 and the company's flagship beer, Molson Canadian, in 1959. By 1971, the company reached 100 million gallons and began to focus on the U.S. market.

In 1989, Molson merged with Foster's Brewing Group and Carling O'Keefe to become Canada's largest brewer and the fifth largest in North America. In 1993, it formed an alliance with Miller Brewing Company. The 1990s also saw the introduction of several new brands, including Canada's first non-alcoholic beers – **Molson Exel** and **Molson Hi Dry.** The company's lineup now includes more than 40 brands of beer.

Brew Stats

Brewer
Molson Canada

Location
Montreal, Canada

First Brewed
1959

Style
Lager

Taste
Smooth and full

Color
Golden

Alcohol Content
5.0%

Ad Campaigns

Molson began advertising early on with its first ad appearing in the *Canadian Courant* in 1807 and its first use of an ad agency in 1930. In 1997, the slogan "what beer's all about!" was introduced in English-speaking Canada, but the successful "I am Canadian" slogan has garnered the most fame. This nationalistic campaign, which was

"I am Canadian" TV ad.

reintroduced in 2000, kicked off early in the year with a television commercial known as "The Rant." It featured Joe Canadian dispelling myths and stereotypes about Canadians. The ad was awarded a Bronze Lion at the International Advertising Festival held in Cannes, France in June 2000.

Molson has also begun to create ads for the United States again. A 2000 campaign features the tagline "there are friends, and there are Molson friends." The two initial ads show a group of friends saying one thing while their implied meanings appear as subtitles on the bottom of the screen. The message is that some friends are too close to be fooled and deserve only the highest quality beer – Molson.

Besides The Beer

A portrait of John Molson Sr.

John Molson Sr. laid the foundation for a multi-million dollar brewing industry. But he didn't stop there. Always the entrepreneur, Molson went on to achieve milestones in several other fields as well. He built Canada's first steamboat, launched in 1809, and later formed the St. Lawrence Steamboat Company, known as the "Molson Line." One of these boats was the first in the world to be used for war purposes. The Molson family also opened two hotels (both of which fell prey to fires) and opened the first industrial Canadian grain distillery. In 1821, Molson helped to found the Montreal General Hospital and heavily invested in Canada's first railroad. In 1855, Molson Bank was chartered and later merged with the Bank of Montreal in 1925.

A Montreal Canadiens hockey player in action.

In 1957, Molson's longstanding relationship with Canada's favorite pastime, hockey, was established when the company co-sponsored Hockey Night. The relationship broadened in 1976 when Molson became Hockey Night's principal sponsor. In 1978, Molson bought the Montreal Canadiens hockey team and in 1996, it opened a sports, business and entertainment facility named the Molson Centre that became the team's new home.

Molson Merchandise

Your Molson retailer is the person who should be able to help you purchase this array of products.

Hat ——

—— Golf Bag

Key Chain ——

Water Bottle ——

T-Shirt

Golf Balls ——

Go to CollectorsQuest.com for more information on Molson Canadian.

Moosehead Beer

Nothing says Canada like the majestic moose. So it's no surprise that Moosehead uses this animal to grace its distinctive label. Just as the moose is a prime target of hunters, this smooth Canadian lager is hunted down by beer drinkers. In fact, it won a gold medal for its high quality standards from Europe's prestigious Monde Selection organization.

A Moosehead neon sign.

Moosehead As A Calf

Moosehead is Canada's oldest independent brewery, formed in Nova Scotia in 1867 when Susannah Oland brewed a batch of brown October ale from a family recipe. The recipe was successful enough that Susannah and her husband John were able to open the Army & Navy Brewery in Halifax. Shortly after, John was killed in an accident and Susannah was left to care for their children. She continued to run the brewery, which she renamed S. Oland Sons & Co. in 1877. After Susannah's death in 1886, her sons took over the family business, which eventually was renamed the Moosehead Brewery.

Halifax

The largest explosion of its time occurred near the site of the Oland brewery in 1917 when two ships, one carrying munitions, collided, causing fires and mass destruction.

Today, Moosehead is run by the fifth generation of the family – chairman and owner Derek Oland. In addition to its Moosehead Canadian Lager, the company makes several brands exclusive to Canada including **Moosehead Light** and **Moosehead Pale Ale**.

"Heed The Call"

But it's not all work and no play. Moosehead's promotions have included a Cabin Fever Rescue program that brings beer to thirsty campers by a miniature bush plane, starting a junior hockey team known as the Halifax Mooseheads and holding a Moosehead Madness event in conjunction with college basketball's March Madness tournament. On the advertising front, the company issued radio and television spots advising Americans to "heed the call" of Moosehead – and many have done just that.

Brew Stats

Brewer
Moosehead
Breweries Limited

Location
St. John, Canada

First Brewed
1948

Style
Canadian Lager

Taste
Smooth, crisp, and well balanced

Color
Golden

Alcohol Content
5.0%

More Moosehead!

In addition to providing information about Moosehead Breweries' products and company history, *www.mooseheadbeer.com* offers a wide selection of merchandise for reasonable prices.

Hat
$6.50

Bottle Opener
$6.00

Key chain
$4.00

Backpack
$50.00

Bucket Hat
$8.50

Portfolio Bag
$85.00

Go to Collectors Quest .com for more information on Moosehead Beer.

Moosehead Beer

Natural Light

Not a lot of dough? Not a problem. If you want to enjoy a great-tasting beer without spending a lot of money, then Natural Light, or "Natty Light" as it has been nicknamed by its fans, is the beer for you!

A Natural Light coaster.

The Natural Choice

Natural Light holds an important spot in the history of Anheuser-Busch because it was the first reduced-calorie, or "light," beer to be offered by the company. It debuted in several test markets in the West and Midwest sections of the United States in early 1977.

Early Natural Light advertisements featured legendary sports figures such as Tommy Lasorda of the Los Angeles Dodgers and hockey great Gordie Howe. The ads were a takeoff on those of Miller Lite, the reigning light beer at the time. In fact, several of Natural Light's ads featured celebrities who had previously endorsed Miller Lite, such as New York Yankee great Mickey Mantle and boxer Joe Frasier. These early ads carried slogans such as "look who switched to Natural Light" and "taste is why you'll switch."

Rest Of The Best

The only beers to outrank Natural Light in total national sales include Bud, Bud Light, Miller Lite, Coors Light and Busch. Fine company indeed!

Changes Are Brewing

Natural Light proved popular among light beer enthusiasts, but, by 1982, a change was in the air at Anheuser-Busch. Natural Light passed the torch to **Bud Light** as Anheuser-Busch's premium light beer. In its new role as a sub-premium beer, Natural Light became the drink of choice for beer fans looking for a truly enjoyable light beer at an affordable price. Although Natural Light may stand in the shadow of Bud Light, its devoted following of loyal supporters have propelled it to a highly respectable sixth-place ranking among all beer brands in 2000.

Like many other Anheuser-Busch beers, Natural Light eventually spawned an off-shoot. **Natural Ice**, a smoothly satisfying ice beer was test marketed in 1995 and became available nationwide in 1996.

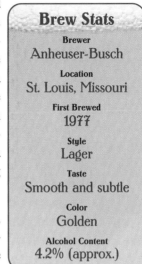

Brew Stats

Brewer
Anheuser-Busch

Location
St. Louis, Missouri

First Brewed
1977

Style
Lager

Taste
Smooth and subtle

Color
Golden

Alcohol Content
4.2% (approx.)

It's Only Natural

Show the world that you're a "natural" by wearing Natural Light gear. You can get yours at *www.budshop.com.*

Hat
$9.00

Long Sleeve Polo
$45.00

Key Chain/
Bottle Opener
$.50

Go to CollectorsQuest.com for more information on Natural Light.

Newcastle Brown Ale

Have you walked the dog today? That's the question Geordies (residents of Newcastle-upon-Tyne, England, home of Newcastle Brown Ale) ask when they're heading to the local pub to have themselves some of their favorite ale, Newcastle Brown Ale. In fact, Newcastle Brown Ale has several affectionate nicknames, including "The Dog,"

Newcastle's packaging plays up the beer's brown color.

"Newkie Broon" and "NBA." It may be called by many names, but as the label says, it is "The One and Only."

Newcastle Brown Ale's favorite-ale status isn't just limited to the hometown crowd, though. It is the #1 bottled beer in the United Kingdom and is gaining ground in the United States, ranking as the #15 imported beer.

The History Of Tyne's Tipple

"Tipple" is slang for any alcoholic beverage and the United Kingdom's largest brewery, Scottish & Newcastle – of which Newcastle Breweries Ltd. is a subsidiary – certainly makes a good one. Newcastle Brown Ale's history began in Newcastle-upon-Tyne's first commercial brewery, John Barras & Company, which was founded in 1770. In 1890 they purchased several breweries in England, including the Tyne Brewery, and formed Newcastle

Is There A Draft In Here?

Although available in draft form for many years elsewhere, 2000 marks the first time that Newcastle Brown Ale became available on draft in the United Kingdom – and only in Newcastle-upon-Tyne.

IMPORTED FROM ENGLAND

12 FL OZ

The One and Only
http://www.newcastlebrown.com
BREWED BY NEWCASTLE BREWERIES LTD, NEWCASTLE UPON TYNE, ENGLAND

NEWCASTLE
SERVE COOL ®
BROWN ALE
IMPORTED BY SCOTTISH & NEWCASTLE IMPORTERS CO., SAN FRANCISCO, CA.

Newcastle is the brown ale of choice for those looking to ease into dark beers.

Breweries Ltd. In 1960 Newcastle Breweries merged with Scottish Brewers to obtain its current moniker – Scottish & Newcastle Breweries.

Newcastle Brown Ale was born in 1927, after three long years of development by Colonel Jim Porter. The following year, Newcastle Brown Ale proceeded to win gold medals at the 1928 International Brewers' Exhibition.

Brew Stats

Brewer
Scottish & Newcastle Breweries.

Location
Newcastle-upon-Tyne, England

First Brewed
1927

Style
Brown Ale

Taste
Sweet, slightly bitter, nutty and tangy

Color
Brown

Alcohol Content
4.7%

Walking The Dog In Style

Lucky for you there is more than just "one and only" one way to show your love for "Newkie Broon." You can get your paws on this merchandise at promotional events.

Polo Shirt

T-Shirt

Hat

Pint Glass

Go to Collectors Quest .com for more information on Newcastle Brown Ale.

Old Milwaukee

It Just Keeps Getting Better

Do you remember the Swedish Bikini Team? These blonde-haired, bikini-clad women found fame in the early 1990s through an advertising campaign for Old Milwaukee beer. In the commercials, a group of men are fishing or hunting or doing general "guy-bonding" activities and having a great time, causing one of them to utter Old Milwaukee's slogan: "It doesn't get any better than this." But things do get better for the guys when the Swedish Bikini Team appears out of nowhere, bringing a supply of Old Milwaukee.

Hog Heaven

Milwaukee is home to the Harley-Davidson manufacturing plant, which is a must-see for visitors to the town. Free tours are available for "hogheads" who want to visit the plant's museum.

Pabst And Present

In 1999, the competitive nature of the beer industry forced Stroh to close its doors after nearly 150 years in the business. Stroh sold many of its brands, including Old Milwaukee, to Pabst Brewing Company, while others were sold to Miller Brewing Company.

There have been few changes to Old Milwaukee other than the name of its corporate owner. It is still brewed at the Lehigh Valley (Pennsylvania) Brewery where it was brewed under Stroh's leadership and its brewmaster is still the same.

And Old Milwaukee is still good beer. Just ask the judges at 1999's Great American Beer Festival, who awarded Old Milwaukee three gold medals, including

one for **Old Milwaukee Light** and one for its non-alcoholic brand. The company's brewmaster, Dan Melideo, received the Large Brewing Company Brewmaster Of The Year award, while Pabst received the Large Brewing Company of the Year award. Not a bad showing at all for Old Milwaukee and its new parent company.

An Old Milwaukee 12-pack.

Other brands in the Pabst portfolio include **Colt 45, Lone Star, Schlitz, Schmidt's,** and **Pabst Blue Ribbon.**

New Gear For Old Milwaukee

There's nothing old about the latest products showcasing Old Milwaukee. To find out how to get yours, go to *www,pabst.com.*

Beverage Wrench
$1.00

Hat
$14.95

T-Shirt —
$10.00

Go to CollectorsQuest.com for more information on Old Milwaukee.

Pacifico Clara

The first thing you are likely to notice about this beer is its eye-catching yellow label and its abundant maritime symbolism. Contained inside a life preserver is a golden anchor while a large mountain stands majestically in the background.

The Grupo Modelo family of beers.

This mountain – located in Mazatlan, Mexico – is home to El Faro, the world's second-highest lighthouse. Upon seeing the seaside theme that graces the Pacifico bottle, it should come as no surprise that this smooth, crisp lager is recommended as the perfect accompaniment to seafood.

Grande Grupo

Pacifico Clara is brewed by Cerveceria del Pacifico – a division of the large Mexican brewers Grupo Modelo. Grupo Modelo was founded in 1925 and currently produces 10 different kinds of beer, five of which – **Corona Extra, Corona Light, Modelo Especial, Negra Modelo** and Pacifico Clara – are exported to 140 different countries, including the United States. Two separate companies import the beer to

Fun Run

December will mark the return of the annual Pacifico Marathon. In 2000, the 26.2-mile race offered $1 million to anyone who broke the world record.

the United States – Barton Beers, Ltd. in the western part of the country and The Gambrinus Company in the eastern part of the country.

Grupo Modelo is the leading beer producer in Mexico with more than half of the export and domestic market share and it owns eight breweries in Mexico. Modelo is the exclusive importer of

Anheuser-Busch products into Mexico and in 1994, the company made its first appearance on the Mexican Stock Exchange.

Pass The Pacifico

This beer, which is among the top-ten best sellers in Mexico, was not introduced into the United States until 1985. At first, it was only available on the West Coast, but its overwhelming popularity prompted Modelo to tap into the East Coast markets as well. Now this beer is well-known across the country and is widely available.

Purchasing Pacifico

Now you can bring Pacifico Clara home with you in more ways than one. Contact your local retailer to find out how to buy jackets, shirts, hats and other assorted merchandise.

Brew Stats

Brewer
Grupo Modelo

Location
Mazatlan, Mexico

First Brewed
N/A

Style
Lager

Taste
Hoppy, smooth and full-flavored

Color
Pale gold

Alcohol Content
4.5%

Hat

Umbrella

Bottle Openers

Jacket

Go to Collectors Quest .com for more information on Pacifico Clara.

Pete's Wicked Ale

Have you even thought of turning your beer-brewing hobby into a business? Well, that's what Pete Slosberg did and now beer drinkers across the nation are happily lifting their glasses of Pete's Wicked Ale in a toast to the founder of Pete's Brewing Company.

Pete Slosberg at work.

The company, which now has facilities on both coasts, had its origins in Slosberg's kitchen. A business executive by day, Slosberg was a home wine vintner by night. After deciding that wine took too long to make, Slosberg started brewing beer at home. He tinkered with his recipe and created Pete's Wicked Ale.

Pete's Wicked Ale and the Pete's Brewing Company made their debut in 1986 to much success. The classic brown ale was welcomed as a craft beer, a beer known for its emphasis on fewer ingredients and no preservatives or additives.

Wicked Good Beer . . .

Disappearing Trick

Can't find your favorite Pete's brand anymore? It isn't a trick – Pete's downsized the number of beers it brews (from twelve to eight) to focus efforts on its best-selling brands.

The Pete's line of beers is brewed at breweries owned by other beer manufacturers (known as contract brewers). The Miller brewery in Eden, North Carolina, and the Pabst brewery in Turnwater, Washington, both serve as contract brewers for Pete's. A Pete's Brewing brewmaster works in conjunction with the breweries to ensure that the recipes are followed and that the resulting product meets Pete's Brewing's standards of excellence.

Since its inception, the Pete's line of beers has been recognized as being among the best in the marketplace; they've won more than 40 national and international quality awards!

The company now has eight beers in its family. The year-round beers are Pete's Wicked Ale, **Pete's Honey Wheat**, **Pete's Pub Lager**, **Pete's Strawberry Blonde** and **Pete's Signature Pilsner**. The seasonal offerings include **Pete's Summer Brew** for the warm-weather months, **Pete's Oktoberfest** for the fall and **Pete's Winter Brew** for the cold-weather months.

Pete's Wicked Ale

. . . And Wicked Good Stuff

Call 1-877-PETE-ALE for your catalog of Pete's Wicked Ale merchandise.

Cooler Bag
$34.25

Fossil Watch
$103.50

Hat
$6.50

Tank Top
$12.50

Go to CollectorsQuest.com for more information on Pete's Wicked Ale.

Pyramid Pale Ale

Visitors to Seattle will find no shortage of things to do and see. From watching one of the local bands in the hot Seattle music scene to dining at the top of the distinctive Space Needle, tourists are sure to keep busy. And all of these

A pile of Pyramid coasters.

activities will prove to be more enjoyable when paired with a Pyramid Pale Ale, which is brewed right in "The Emerald City" itself.

Building The Pyramid

Pyramid Pale Ale's history dates back to 1984, when Hart Brewing was founded in an old general store in the small logging town of Kalama, Washington. As the company added more beers to its repertoire, the general store proved much too small. The company moved to a larger facility in Kalama in 1992 before relocating for a second time in 1995 – this time to the Seattle brewery and alehouse that it still maintains today. Located across the street from Safeco Field, home to Major League Baseball's Seattle Mariners, the brewery now distributes its beer to more than 30 states as well as Canada and Japan.

Following the move to Seattle, Hart Brewing changed its name to Pyramid Breweries and in 1997, the company opened a

Party With Pyramid

Both Pyramid breweries host an annual Let It Flow, Let It Snow party that features local bands, good food, games (a dunk in the beer tank is popular) and, of course, plenty of Pyramid beer.

Have a good beer.

Every beer deserves a good home.

A Pyramid bookmark.

second brewery and alehouse in Berkeley, California, to keep up with distribution demands. This brewery, housed in an old Greyhound bus building, produces more than 80,000 barrels of beer annually, which keeps students (of legal drinking age, of course) and faculty at the nearby University of California at Berkeley happy, especially before UC-Berkeley football games and during "Outdoor Cinema" nights, when classic movies are shown on the brewery's wall.

More Great Pyramids

In addition to its Pale Ale, Pyramid Breweries has 10 other beers, including **Hefeweizen**, **Alehouse ESB**, **Apricot Ale**, **Best Brown**, **India Pale Ale** and **Wheaten Ale**, as well as the seasonal **Tilted Kilt,** **Sun Fest**, **Broken Rake** and **Snow Cap**.

Brew Stats

Brewer
Pyramid Breweries Inc.

Location
Seattle, Washington

First Brewed
1984

Style
Pale ale

Taste
Nutty-malt

Color
Copper

Alcohol Content
5.1%

Passionate About Pyramid?

A plethora of Pyramid products can be bought through *www.pyramidales.com.* Items without prices are promotional items.

Hat
$14.95

T-Shirt

Go to Collectors Quest.com for more information on Pyramid Pale Ale.

Redhook IPA

What Seattle-based brewery can boast that all of its products are kosher? The answer is the Redhook Ale Brewery. Redhook, which has been brewing quality beer since 1981, submitted its nine beers for kosher certification in 1999 to prove to

A postcard of Seattle's Redhook Ale Brewery.

its customers that it uses only the freshest ingredients. In addition to adherence to the Jewish religion, kosher products contain fewer additives and preservatives. So, the next time you're in the mood for great-tasting quality beer, pick up a Redhook!

How It All Began

The Redhook Ale Brewery was the brainstorm of Paul Shipman and Gordon Bowker, who felt that people in the Seattle region would appreciate a finely crafted European-style beer. In just 15 months, the pair presented their first beer to Seattle. It was a failure. But Shipman and Bowker persisted and introduced a second beer, **Blackhook Porter**, the following year, which is still produced and sold today.

Hail To The Trolleyman

Redhook's Seattle brewery is in a building once used as a trolley car barn. In honor of the building and the people who worked there, the Redhook brewery named its brewpub Trolleyman.

It was their third offering, in 1984, that put Redhook on the map. Ballard Bitter, now known as Redhook IPA, took the city by storm. People all over Seattle were not only drinking it, but also passing along the word to their friends.

INDIA PALE ALE

IPA

"YA SURE" "YA BETCHA"

BALLARD BITTER

Contents
12 Fluid

A New Home For Brew

Shipman and Bowker moved to the former home of the Seattle Electric Railway to keep up with the demand for Ballard Bitter. The new Redhook brewery opened in September 1988 and was closely followed by additional Redhook breweries in Woodinville, Washington and on the East Coast in Portsmouth, New Hampshire.

While Redhook IPA was the original success of the brewery, Redhook Breweries offers a wide variety of year-round and seasonal products. Also included in the Redhook family are **Redhook ESB**, **Hefeweizen, Doubleblack Stout, Nut Brown Ale**, **Blonde Ale** and **Winterhook Ale.**

Brew Stats

Brewer
Redhook Ale Brewery

Location
Seattle, Washington

First Brewed
1984

Style
India pale ale

Taste
Aggressively hopped, dry, crisp finish

Color
Brass

Alcohol Content
6.5%

Hooked On Redhook

Pay a visit to the Redhook Ale Brewery's official web site at *www.redhook.com* to find out how to lure these items into your home.

Hat —
$12.00

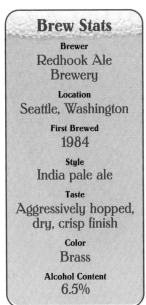

Polo Shirt
$38.00

T-Shirt —
14.00

Hat —
$12.00

Pint Glass
$5.00

Go to CollectorsQuest.com for more information on Redhook IPA.

Rolling Rock Extra Pale

Latrobe, Pennsylvania is the birthplace of many American icons. Children's television pioneer Mister Rogers was born there in 1928. Golfer Arnold Palmer was born there in 1929. And Rolling Rock Extra Pale was invented there by the Latrobe Brewing Company in 1939.

The Latrobe Brewery in Latrobe, Pennsylvania.

Latrobe is located at the base of the Allegheny Mountains, southeast of Pittsburgh. Brewed from fresh mountain spring water from Pennsylvania's Laurel Highlands, Rolling Rock gets its name from the smooth stones found in the streams that serve as the spring's source.

Marketing Might

Rolling Rock is as well known for its distinctive packaging as for its great taste. Its painted-on label and green glass bottle set it apart from other beers. The painted-on label won't slip off when wet, like glued-on labels, and it also helps Rolling Rock drinkers get a better grip on the bottle.

The back of the label contains Rolling Rock's pledge to its drinkers followed by the number "33." The Latrobe Brewing Company won't reveal what that number implies, but Rolling Rock philosophers have suggested that it may relate to the number of words in the pledge, the year Prohibition was repealed or the temperature at which the beer tastes best.

In their print advertisements, Rolling Rock discusses the fine ingredients that go into their beer, while

The Green Bottle

During World War II, bars returned empty beer bottles to their breweries to reuse. Rolling Rock's distinctive green bottles made them easy to identify from the others.

166

simultaneously encouraging drinkers to be responsible about drinking and driving.

A Rolling Rock print advertisement.

The Tito 5

The Latrobe Brewing Company formed in the 1890s and brewed until Prohibition forced it out of business in the 1920s. The building and its famous glass-lined tanks stood empty for about 10 years, until Frank Tito and his four brothers bought it with the hope that Prohibition would soon end. Their dream came true in 1933. They also created **Latrobe Pilsner** and **Latrobe Old German**, but it was Rolling Rock that made them famous.

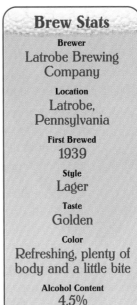

Brew Stats

Brewer
Latrobe Brewing Company

Location
Latrobe, Pennsylvania

First Brewed
1939

Style
Lager

Taste
Golden

Color
Refreshing, plenty of body and a little bite

Alcohol Content
4.5%

Roll Out The Gear

You can get these products from *www.rollingrock.com*. The availability of these items can vary from season to season.

T-Shirt

Hat

Sweatshirt

Go to Collectors Quest .com for more information on Rolling Rock Extra Pale.

St. Pauli Girl

Who would have guessed that the blonde barmaid with the low-cut dress who adorns each can and bottle of St. Pauli Girl Beer has a connection with a monastery? But believe it or not, she has her origins in the St. Pauli Monastery in Bremen, Germany, as the St. Pauli Brewery was built in the 17th century on the grounds of the ancient religious center.

A classic St. Pauli Girl beer can.

Bremen is recognized as the home of German beer and the fine beverage has been brewed there since the 12th century. The beer that first came out of Bremen's St. Pauli Brewery was sold only in cities and was delivered to townspeople straight out of the wooden keg. However, as sea voyages became easier and more widespread, the word began to spread about St. Pauli's beer and the beer traveled to ports along the North Sea.

Radishes And Beer

What's that peeking out of the St. Pauli Girl's apron on old-time St. Pauli Girl Beer cans? Why, they're radishes – a classic accompaniment to German beer!

Birth Of The St. Pauli Girl

It wasn't until the 19th century that the word "Girl" was added to the St. Pauli name. At that time, the use of labels on bottles of beer became more prevalent, and the St. Pauli Brewery wanted to go with the trend. They commissioned an artist to design a label that would have worldwide appeal and would not have too many words. Legend has it that the artist was inspired by the beauty of a local barmaid and it is her image that graces the cans and bottles of the brew and gave the beer its name.

Germany's Fun-Loving Beer

St. Pauli Girl often uses the tagline "fun-loving" to describe itself, and that attitude is reflected in its advertising. A recent billboard promotion for St. Pauli Girl featured the theme "Girls rule. Guys drool." to advertise the beer.

If it's not the beer itself that the guys are drooling over, it might be the young woman who personifies the St. Pauli Girl. Each year a beautiful woman is chosen to represent St. Pauli Girl Beer. Among her duties as the St. Pauli Girl is to appear in St. Pauli Girl advertising. The 2001 St. Pauli Girl is a 1994 Playboy Playmate.

Brew Stats

Brewer
St. Pauli Brewery

Location
Bremen, Germany

First Brewed
1800s

Style
Lager

Taste
Rich, full-bodied

Color
Deep gold

Alcohol Content
4.9%

Show Off Your St. Pauli Girl

The beautiful St. Pauli Girl isn't just limited to appearances on cans, bottles and billboards. You can find her yourself on official caps and T-shirts at *www.stpauligirl.com* or *www.pubshop.com*.

Hat
$16.00

Hat
$18.00

T-Shirt
$18.00

Go to Collectors Quest.com for more information on St. Pauli Girl.

Samuel Adams Boston Lager

The Boston Beer Company boasts that its Samuel Adams beer is the "best beer in America." And for good reason. Samuel Adams beer has won more awards than any other brewery. The brewery that makes Samuel Adams has won top honors for 14 consecutive years at the Great American Beer Festival!

A Samuel Adams neon sign.

There are 13 different kinds of Samuel Adams beers brewed by the Boston Beer Company and Boston Lager is probably the most popular year-round beer. **Boston Ale**, **Cherry Wheat**, **Cream Stout**, **Golden Pilsner**, **IPA**, **Pale Ale** and **Triple Bock** round out the always-available offerings. **Winter Lager** is on store shelves from October through February, **Double Bock** and **Spring Ale** are available from January through March, **Summer Ale** can be purchased from May through August and **Octoberfest** is available from August through October.

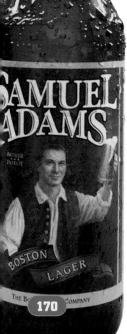

About Samuel Adams:

1. Don't confuse him with John Adams, the second president of the United States. They were cousins.

2. Don't ever call him "Sam." Only his enemies called him that.

The remaining beer is **Samuel Adams Millennium**, billed as a "once-in-a-lifetime beer." It was brewed especially for the turn of the millennium and only 3,000 bottles were made. They were each signed by Boston Beer Company founder Jim Koch and numbered. Look for this special beer (its alcohol percentage hovers close to 20%) in a blue bottle with platinum lettering and packaged in a cherry wood box.

A Family Tradition

Jim Koch comes from a long line of brewmasters – in fact, he's the fifth generation of Koch men to take on the career. His great-great grandfather, Louis, first brewed beer in Germany and kept it up when he immigrated to the United States. He founded the Louis

One of the Samuel Adams delivery trucks.

Koch Brewery in St. Louis, where he made Louis Koch Lager. The brewery was successful for more than 20 years, but found it couldn't hold off the competition. Industry giant Anheuser-Busch had its operations just blocks away.

Charles Jerome Koch, Louis' son, worked as a brewmaster at several St. Louis breweries. His son, Charles Joseph, took a scholarly route and trained at the Siebel Institute, a brewmaster's school. He is credited with inventing and patenting a malt process for beer-making.

His son, Charles Joseph Jr., also trained at the Siebel Institute, but he eventually walked away from the beer industry as industry giants started to squeeze small family breweries out of contention.

A New Generation

Fortunately for Samuel Adams fans, the Koch family involvement did not end with Jim Koch's father. In 1983, Jim Koch left behind his lucrative career as a management consultant and formed the Boston Beer Company. He named his beer after legendary Boston patriot Samuel Adams. His first beer, Samuel Adams Boston Lager, premiered on (appropriately enough) Patriot's Day, a Massachusetts holiday commemorating the Battle of Lexington and Concord. The rest is history.

Brew Stats

Brewer
The Boston Beer Company

Location
Boston, Massachusetts

First Brewed
1985

Style
Lager

Taste
Malty and slightly sweet

Color
Golden amber

Alcohol Content
4.75%

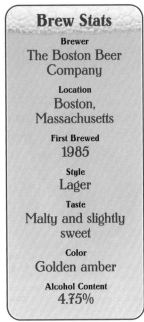

Who Was Samuel Adams?

Born in Boston in 1722, Samuel Adams was the Harvard-educated son of a Boston brewer and a brewmaster himself. He spent more time working with political activist groups than he did working alongside his father, however. He belonged to the Sons of Liberty, a group devoted to educating the public about the evils of English rule, and is credited as one of the leading instigators of the Boston Tea Party in 1773, an act that directly led to the American Revolution. Adams went on to sign the Declaration of Independence in 1776 and become governor of the commonwealth of Massachusetts in 1794.

Sign Of The Times

The signature found on each bottle of Samuel Adams beer is a replica of Samuel Adams' actual signature on the Declaration of Independence.

Samuel Adams . . . Brewed All Over

The Boston Beer Company is headquartered in Boston but has breweries located throughout the United States. You can find Samuel Adams beer that has been brewed in Boston; Cincinnati; Pittsburgh; Portland, Oregon; Rochester, New York or Lehigh Valley, Pennsylvania.

Because of the company's widespread brewing facilities, you can purchase Samuel Adams beer in any of the 50 states. It is imported to the Canadian provinces of British Columbia and Ontario and even to countries as far away as Guam, Hong Kong and Japan!

The Boston Beer Company's worldwide popularity ranks it among the top 10 biggest brewers in the United States. Taste a Samuel Adams Boston Lager today and find out why!

A Samuel Adams coaster features Samuel Adams himself enjoying a mug of beer.

All-American Gear

What better way to show the world your patriotism than through the red, white and blue merchandise of "the best beer in America?" These items and more can be found at *www.samadams.com*. Items without prices are promotional items.

Divot Puller and
Ball Markers

Tees

Pint Glass
(set of 4)
$20.00

Golf Balls

Hat
$9.95

T-Shirt
$12.95

Pitcher

Go to CollectorsQuest.com for more
information on Samuel Adams Boston Lager.

Saranac Pale Ale

The F.X. Matt Brewing Company is a family-owned brewery that has been in operation at the foothills of the Adirondack Mountains in upstate Utica, New York for more than 100 years. Now in its fourth generation of Matt family leadership, Saranac still brews its beer in the slow manner that F.X. Matt used in his first batch of Matt Brewing Company beer in 1888.

The F.X. Matt Brewery has stood in Utica, New York for more than 100 years.

A Cluster Of Beers

Saranac beers are available in nearly 20 states, most of which are located in the Northeast and Mid-Atlantic states. The beer is brewed using fresh mountain water and locally grown grains. Pale Ale is the flagship brand of the company, which also brews **Adirondack Amber**, **Black Forest**, **Black & Tan**, **Pilsener** and **Traditional Lager**. Saranac also brews a variety of seasonal beers, including **Belgian White**, **Chocolate Amber**, **I.P.A.**, **Maple Porter**, **Mountain Berry Ale**, **Wild Berry Wheat** and **Winter Wassail** as well as non-alcoholic beer, regular and diet root beer, and ginger beer.

What Is Saranac Anyway?

The name "Saranac" comes from an Iroquois word that means "cluster of stars." It is also the name of a nearby lake in New York.

Four Generations Of Beer

In 1885, Francis Xavier Matt arrived in the United States from Germany, leaving behind his career at the prestigious Duke of Baden Brewery. F.X. opened the West End Brewing Company in 1888. There were 11

A Saranac table tent.

other breweries operating in Utica at the time, but F.X. was not concerned. F.X. continued at the helm of the brewery until 1951, when his sons Walter and Frank took over.

The modern era of the Matt Brewing Company began with F.X. Matt II, company chairman. F.X. II's brother, Nicholas, joined the business in the late 1980s. As company president, he is responsible for extending the line of Saranac brands and specialty products. Fred Matt, F.X. II's son, is the Vice President of Marketing and Sales.

Brew Stats

Brewer
F.X. Matt Brewing Company

Location
Utica, New York

First Brewed
N/A

Style
English pale ale

Taste
Rich, fruity and crisp

Color
Copper amber

Alcohol Content
5.7% (approx.)

So Much Saranac, So Little Time

Saranac has a wide variety of items available for purchase. There is a store at the Matt Family Brewery where you can start your collection today!

Pint Glass
$2.95

Hat
$12.95

Go to CollectorsQuest.com for more information on Saranac Pale Ale.

175

Shiner Bock

Big things are happening in the small town of Shiner, Texas. Here, approximately 8,000 cases and 500 kegs of Shiner beer are shipped out each day to thirsty Americans around the country.

The Spoetzl Brewery in Shiner, Texas.

And it is here that one of Spoetzl Brewery's most anticipated events, Bocktoberfest, is held each year. The all-day festival, which recently celebrated its seventh year, features a number of Texas musicians and there's always plenty of the #1 bock beer in the United States, Shiner Bock, on hand. Bock is a dark beer that is generally strong with a very malty taste that can also taste chocolatey.

The Story of Spoetzl

Located between Houston and San Antonio, Shiner was founded in 1887 by Czech and German farmers. After several years on the Texas plains, the immigrants longed for the beer of their homeland, so in 1909 they formed the Shiner Brewing Association. Kosmos Spoetzl, a German brewmaster, bought the company in 1915 and history was made. In fact, Kosmos' recipes are still used today and Spoetzl is celebrated as the oldest independent brewery in the state of Texas.

Near Beer

During Prohibition, Spoetzl stayed in business by manufacturing a "near beer." This was accomplished by making real beer and then boiling out the alcohol.

Although Spoetzl is now owned by The Gambrinus Company of San Antonio, an importer of Corona and

A Shiner coaster portrays Texas pride through the outline of the state and a longhorn symbol.

Moosehead beers, the brewery still maintains a small-town feel. All of its beers are brewed in the original Shiner brewery under the supervision of longtime brewmaster John Hybner.

Brew Stats

Brewer
Spoetzl Brewing Company

Location
Shiner, Texas

First Brewed
N/A

Style
Bock

Taste
Rich, full-flavored

Color
Amber

Alcohol Content
4.4%

Shiner In The South

Spoetzl knows the hidden dangers that lie in national distribution. For that reason, its products can only be found in the southern United States. In addition to Shiner Bock, the Spoetzl family includes **Blonde**, **Winter Ale**, **Summer Stock** and **Honey Wheat**, which won a silver medal at 1999's Great American Beer Festival.

Take A Shine To Shiner

Show your friends what your favorite bock beer is with this great Shiner Bock gear. It's available at *www.shiner.com*.

Hat
$12.50

Baseball Jersey
$38.50

Hat
$15.50

Hat
$12.50

Mouse Pad
$11.00

Go to CollectorsQuest.com for more information on Shiner Bock.

Sierra Nevada Pale Ale

While its name is drawn from the impressive mountains which cover parts of eastern California, the Sierra Nevada Brewing Company is actually located in the nearby college town of Chico. Founded by Ken Grossman and Paul Camusi in 1981, the brewery managed to find success in a time when craft beers were virtually unheard of. It has since sustained that success through the rise and fall of the craft-brewing craze of the 1980s and 1990s.

The Sierra Nevada Brewery in Chico, California.

In fact, growth for Sierra Nevada has been so extensive that the company added a second brewery to its forces in 1998 – this one twice the size of the first. As both breweries are now functioning simultaneously, output has increased dramatically, making it easier to produce and distribute beer to nearly every state.

Could It Happen To You?

Ken Grossman and Paul Camusi were friends and home-brewers who were able to turn their hobby into a lucrative career. How about you? Care to give it a try?

The Taste Of Success

The reason for Sierra Nevada's overwhelming success becomes evident when you take your first sip of any one of their great-tasting beers. Their flagship Pale Ale is known for its abundant use of hops, which gives it a sharp aroma and flavor. Sierra Nevada Pale Ale has been named a Gold Medal winner several times over at the nation's most prestigious beer festival, the Great American Beer Festival.

The Sierra Seven

While the Pale Ale remains its most popular brew, six other award-winning beers have joined the Sierra Nevada family, including **Porter**, **Stout** and **Wheat**. There are also two seasonal beers, **Celebration Ale** for the winter holidays and **Summerfest** for the warmer months. **Bigfoot** is Sierra Nevada's barley-wine-style ale.

This Sierra Nevada coaster is as green as the mountains for which the beer is named.

Brew Stats

Brewer
Sierra Nevada
Brewing Company

Location
Chico, California

First Brewed
1981

Style
Pale ale

Taste
Spicy, full-flavored

Color
Deep amber

Alcohol Content
5.6%

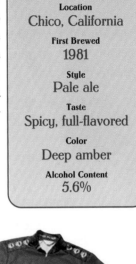

See The Sierras

Everyone can visit Sierra Nevada with a virtual trip to the brewery at *www.sierranevadabeer.com*. This fine merchandise can also be found at *www.sierranevada.com*. Pieces without prices are promotional items.

Bike Jersey
$69.99

Hat

T-Shirt
$12.00

Go to Collectors Quest.com for more information on Sierra Nevada Pale Ale.

Sierra Nevada Pale Ale

Tecate

Saying Tecate (pronounced *ta-ka-tee*) feels as good as it does when you drink it. First launched as a beer for exporting to the United States, Tecate has become one of the most successful brands in Mexico.

A Tecate coaster bears the beer's emblem.

Tecate is a lager beer with aromatic malt and hops that give it a refreshingly subtle taste. A taste that's been a particular favorite, evident in its winning Le Monde Selection's medals: four gold and one silver.

Until 1954, Tecate was brewed by Cervecería Tecate under Don Alberto V. Aldrete. After a series of acquisitions and name changes, the brewery became known as Cervecería Cuauhtémoc Moctezuma, which today falls under the FEMSA umbrella. Besides Tecate, other tantalizing beers that are manufactured by FEMSA include: **Tecate Light**, **Noche Buena**, **Superior, Sol**, **Indio**, **Bohemia**, **Carta Blanca**, **XX Ambar** and **XX Lager**.

The packaging of Tecate has gone through several changes since its inception. In 1956, consumers saw the flip-top, non-refundable can. This was followed by the two-pieces can, non-returnable bottle, ecologically-friendly cap and twist-off bottle cap. In 1991, Tecate became the first to introduce a Mexican 12-pack. Today, Tecate is sold in over 35 nations worldwide and is imported to the United States by Labatt USA.

Can It

In 1953, Tecate was introduced to the Mexican market. Not only was this a big first for Tecate, it was also a big first for Mexico as Tecate became its first canned beer.

180

Race To The Border

Tecate has not only made its presence well known on the beer scene, but also the racing scene as well. Known for its sponsorship in motor racing, as well as of famous

Indy Car Racer, Adrian Fernandez, Tecate is a fast moving brew in many ways. For more information, check out the *www.femsa.com* official web site.

A Tecate six-pack.

Brew Stats

Brewer
Cervecería
Chauhtémoc
Moctezuma

Location
Tecate, Mexico

First Brewed
1944

Style
Lager

Taste
Balanced

Color
Golden

Alcohol Content
4.5% (approx.)

I'll Take Tecate

Here is a sampling of some of the great products that have the Tecate logo. These items are for promotional purposes only and are not available for purchase.

— Polo Shirt

Key Chain

Go to CollectorsQuest.com for more information on Tecate.

Widmer Brothers Hefeweizen

America's original Hefeweizen, is a taste of Europe brewed in Portland, Oregon, USA. Part of a family-run business, Hefeweizen is brewed by brothers Kurt and Rob Widmer and is the flagship beer of the Widmer Brothers Brewing Company. Other members of the award-winning brewing family include **Hop Jack Pale Ale**, **Sweet Betty Blonde Ale**, **Widberry**, **Altbier**, and the popular seasonal brews **Springfest**, **Sommerbrau**, **Oktoberfest** and **Winternacht**.

The Widmer Brothers brewery in Portland, Oregon.

The brothers were inspired to go into the beer business in the mid-1980s, when Kurt returned to the United States after living in Germany. He decided to try his hand at brewing authentic European beer unlike any other in the United States. He returned to Germany briefly, to study recipes in Düsseldorf and to obtain special brewing yeast from the Brewing Research Institute in Weihenstephan, Bavaria. The Widmer Brothers brewery continues to use that yeast even today.

The beer itself is brewed in a special way. As it is bottled directly from the lagering tank and not filtered, this special yeast will actually remain suspended in the beer. You can see the result of this suspension in the beer's cloudy appearance.

Secret To Success

From the beginning, the brother's used a yeast that they got from the internationally famous Brewing Research Institute in Weihenstephan, Bavaria.

A Family Affair

Print advertisements for "America's Original Hefeweizen" focus on the fact that it is a family-run business. And to reinforce that ideal, the ads even refer to the children as "wheat" and "barley."

A Widmer Brothers print advertisement.

Brew Stats

Brewer
Widmer Brothers Brewing Company

Location
Portland, Oregon

First Brewed
1986

Style
Hefeweizen

Taste
Slightly bitter

Color
Golden

Alcohol Content
4.7%

Family Loyalty

You can find this sample of products, as well as much more, on the official Widmer Brothers web site *www.widmer.com.*

Polo Shirt
$35.00

Glass
$4.00

Hat
$10.00

T-Shirt (back)
$12.00

Go to CollectorsQuest.com for more information on Widmer Brothers Hefeweizen.

Yuengling Porter

Pottsville, Pennsylvania, may appear to be an unassuming location on the map, but since 1829, the hilly town has been home to a booming brewery business. In fact, no other brewery in the United States has been brewing beer longer than Yuengling (pronounced *ying-ling*). Canada's Molson

The D.G. Yuengling and Son brewery.

Breweries might have quibbled that they are North America's oldest brewery, but the United States Patent and Trademark Office determined that the Pennsylvania plant can proudly proclaim itself "America's Oldest Brewery."

The Yuengling family brewery which was originally established in 1829 under the name Eagle, was destroyed by fire in 1831. Soon after, the Yuenglings rebuilt nearby and the brewery still stands today. In 1873, company founder David G. Yuengling was joined in the business by his son Frederick, and the Eagle Brewery appropriately became D.G. Yuengling and Son to reflect this change.

No Stopping Yuengling

Prohibition, fire and megabreweries have not been able to destroy D.G. Yuengling, which has become a symbol of Pennsylvanian perseverance. The brewery's survival is based upon its ability to maintain its historical roots while embracing progress.

Yuengling has been so successful in recent years that it has been faced with scaling back the number of states in which its products are available. The brew-

The Eagle Still Flies

Although the days of the Eagle Brewery are now past, the memories live on in the image of the eagle who spreads his wings in triumph on the labels of the bottles of Yuengling Porter.

ery simply couldn't keep up with the demand for its product, even at yearly production of more than half a million barrels.

In an effort to increase production, a new Yuengling brewery has been built in Pottsville (the original brewery will continue to brew beer and conduct visitor tours). Yuengling has also purchased a former Stroh's brewery in Florida that should also aid greatly in production.

Yuengling has been producing a porter since 1873, and they have no plans to stop. The Yuengling family still owns their historic brewery and if fifth-generation Yuengling, Dick, has his way, his daughters will one day proudly lead the brewery into even greater prosperity.

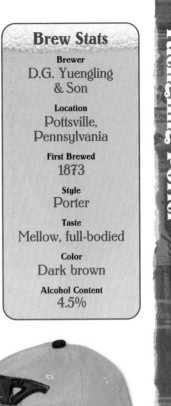

Brew Stats

Brewer
D.G. Yuengling & Son

Location
Pottsville, Pennsylvania

First Brewed
1873

Style
Porter

Taste
Mellow, full-bodied

Color
Dark brown

Alcohol Content
4.5%

Have An Inkling For Yuengling?

Yuengling clothing is available for purchase at *www.yuengling.com.* Get yours now!

Hat
$11.99

T-Shirt
$7.99

Go to Collectors Quest.com for more information on Yuengling Porter.

What's Brewing On The Secondary Market

Collecting beer memorabilia, or breweriana, has become quite popular. No matter how much you have collected, it may seem like you never have enough. There are always those rare and special pieces that you just can't live without. The tricky part is finding them, and that's what the secondary market is for.

What Is Collectible?

Since so many collectibles are available, many people specialize and focus on certain types of items for their collection. Some people only collect certain products like coasters or steins. Others collect items for a specific brand like Budweiser or Coors. Some even specialize by region like Boston or England.

There are also many reasons to collect. Some pieces, such as cans and packaging, tell a history. Others, such as tap handles and trays, are beautifully crafted. And many of these pieces are very hard to find. Just think of how many cocktail napkins and beer cans you have thrown away.

A sample of Budweiser collectibles.

Where Is The Secondary Market?

Perhaps the most useful innovation to affect the secondary market is the Internet. There are several options, including bidding in on-line auctions, viewing the stock at an on-line store, buying from someone's personal collection or trading through an exchange. Contacting other collectors through chat rooms, mailing lists and bulletin boards will also provide you with shopping opportunities. By typing "beer collectibles" or "breweriana" into a search engine, you should find many useful web pages. Just remember to always exercise caution when dealing on the Internet.

Also, don't forget about print resources. You may want to check your local newspaper for regional events and want ads. There are also many specialized beer publications, full of announcements for shows, conventions, auctions, want ads and store advertisements.

Joining a collector's club is another great way to get in touch with other collectors, flesh out your collection and stay informed about events. You should also check your phone book for specialty and antique stores in your area.

What Is It Worth?

Fink's Off The Wall Auctions is one type of print resource.

Several factors can affect a collectible's market value including condition, variations, age and rarity. As with any collectible item, the condition of your breweriana is very important. Be sure to look for specialized products that will help you remove things like caps and labels without damaging them. You can find special storage products like shelving, wall mountings or albums to accommodate and protect any type of collection.

Some items, like coasters, may have subtle variations that are coveted by other collectors. Identifying the age of your piece can involve researching the brewery and its history, and finding out about the various manufacturing specifics will help to pin down a date. Also remember that rarity is a factor. When there are fewer pieces available than there are collectors who want them, the value of these pieces can skyrocket.

There are some items of breweriana – bottles, bottle caps and labels, for example – that don't have much secondary market value. Their value is more of a personal nature, as collectors of these items generally save them as momentos or souvenirs of good times and special vacations.

Just about anything can be a collectible.

On the following pages, we introduce you to breweriana collectors who've shared some of their collections with us. We've calculated secondary market prices for most of their pieces to help you understand how valuable some of your breweriana items may be.

Bottle Caps

Bottle caps are an inexpensive way to start a breweriana collection, and they are very colorful to display. Alan Reed-Erickson fell

into collecting beer bottle caps by default. Ten years ago he started collecting beer bottles. Due to space limitations, he reduced his collecting to labels and bottle caps.

Alan Reed-Erickson's bottle cap collection is a history of the beer he has tasted.

Reed-Erickson does not belong to any formal collecting associations nor does he buy his bottle tops at conventions or antique stores. He has his own method of collecting. During his travels, Reed-Erickson visits specialty beer stores and breweries to find unusual beers which he has not tasted before. Unless he has tasted the beer first, he will not add the new bottle caps to his collection .

At present, Reed-Erickson has approximately 750 pieces in his bottle cap collection. He displays his collection by attaching the caps to a push-pin and tacking them on a bul-

Miller High Life
Miller Brewing
Company
Milwaukee, WI

letin board. His hobby is also a way for him to track his travels, which gives his collection a highly personal value.

Original Coors
Coors Brewing
Company
Golden, CO

Collecting Bottle Caps

Bottle caps (or "crowns") are a subcategory of breweriana that do not fetch very high values on the secondary market, as they are items of a more personal nature. It can be tricky to collect caps that you need a bottle opener to remove, as the opener will likely ruin the cap. In lieu of smashing the bottle apart, try placing a coin or other metal object between the cap and the opener when removing non-screw off caps. The coin should take the brunt of the abuse, leaving the cap in good condition.

The Three
Stooges Beer
Panther Brewing Co.
Westwood, MA

Blue Moon
Brewing Co.
Golden, CO

August Schell
Brewing Co.
New Ulm, MN

Budweiser
Anheuser-Busch
St. Louis, MO

Flying Dog Brewpub
Aspen, CO

Harp Lager
Harp Lager Brewery
Dundalk, Ireland

Grolsch Mei Bok
Grolsch Brewery
Groenlo, Netherlands

Bottle Openers

John Stanley is an avid bottle opener collector. He started in 1977 when his mother gave him about 25 antique bottle openers. This gift sparked his interest and he started collecting more openers. Today he has roughly 3,000 soda and beer bottle openers, of which approximately 2,000 are beer-related.

Bottle openers are categorized by an alpha-numeric system invented by Don Bull in the 1970s. According to this system, there are 900 types of bottle openers.

Stanley has two themes in his collection. His first goal is to obtain a piece to represent each and every one of the 900 different types of bottle openers. His second is to gather a smaller collection of bottle openers from regional breweries.

Bottle openers can be found at a variety of venues, such as garage sales, flea markets, conventions, antique stores and Internet auctions. An innovative and exciting new way of collecting is through a mail exchange. Users of a mail exchange receive a printed list of bottle openers. To obtain a piece that someone else has, you simply exchange a part of your collection with that person by mail.

Stanley feels that bottle opener collecting is an affordable hobby. Currently, bottle openers range in price anywhere from 25¢ to $1,000, the majority of which can be purchased for less than $50.

Herman Lackman
Brewery
Germantown, OH
1911
Value: $100

Circa dates of bottle openers provided by John Stanley.

Collecting Bottle Openers

Bottle openers are a great item for novice breweriana collectors to collect because they are small and therefore relatively easy to store. They come in all shapes and sizes, are interesting to look at and have demand on the secondary market. Notice how some of these bottle openers have a square hole on them? That was used to turn on the gas headlights of cars from about 1910 through the 1920s before electric headlights were widely used.

Medford Lager
Medford Brewing Co.
Medford, WI
1933-1940
Value: $95

Pabst Blue Ribbon
Pabst Brewing Co.
Chicago, IL
Patented 1904
Value: $140

Miller High Life
Miller Brewing Co.
Milwaukee, WI
1933-1940
Value: $55

P. Ballantine & Sons
Ballantine Beer
Newark, NJ
1910-1920
Value: $150

Narragansett Lager
Narragansett Beer
Cranston, RI
1910-1920
Value: $195

Falls City Beer
Falls City Brewing Co.
Louisville, KY
1933-1940
Value: $110

Tech Beer
Pittsburgh Brewing Co.
Pittsburgh, PA
1916
Value: $125

Bottles

It is very hard to separate the collector from the connoisseur when talking with Dan Baker. He is a collector of "beer experiences" as well as beer bottles. His beer travels have taken him to far away places like Viarme, France and Fredrikstad, Norway.

Dan Baker's collection is much more than just bottles.

Although Baker cannot recall exactly when he started collecting, he recalls that a course he took as a graduate student in college seemed to intensify his interest in beer. For this course, Baker had to choose an unknown area and study the development of learning. So, Baker chose to learn how to make beer. He has been making his own beer ever since and considers this hobby to be very complementary to his bottle collecting.

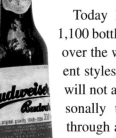

Today his collection numbers roughly 1,100 bottles. His collection comes from all over the world and represents many different styles and methods of brewing. Baker will not add a beer to his collection that he has not personally tasted and catalogued. Each bottle goes through a formal reviewing process. He takes careful notes of the attributes that each beer displays and then enters them in a database that he has designed on his home computer. Baker inputs his beer data by beer name, country of origin and brewing style. Only at this point is the bottle allowed to join its brethren on the display shelf.

Apollo Space-Crafted Ale
Big Bang Brewery
San Francisco, CA

Budweiser
Budweiser Budvar
Ceske Budejovice,
Czechoslovakia

Collecting Bottles

Beer bottles are a fun category of breweriana, although they generally don't have high values on the secondary market. They are considered by many to be difficult to collect because they take up a lot of room and are very susceptible to breaking. The people who do collect bottles tend to do so either because they find the bottles interesting to look at or because the bottles remind them of good times and exciting travels – things that you just can't assign a value to!

Jack Daniel's
Amber Lager
Jack Daniel's Brewery
Lynchburg, TN

Stegmaier 1857
Dry Beer
The Lion Brewery
Wilkes-Barre, PA

Hammer & Nail
Vienna Style Lager
Hammer & Nail
Brewers
Watertown, CT

Coal Porter
The Atlantic Brewing
Company
Bar Harbor, ME

Yuengling Porter
D.G. Yuengling & Son
Pottsville, PA

Budweiser Collection

Talk with Andrew Crumpley for a few minutes about his Anheuser-Busch collection, and you will be at a loss for words. The

Andrew Crumpley has a staggering collection of Anheuser-Busch breweriana.

dedication, passion and fervor that this man from Elk Grove, California, exhibits toward his collecting hobby is nothing short of amazing.

Crumpley remembers starting to collect breweriana in 1988. His employer at the time gave each employee a Budweiser Christmas stein. He decided he liked collecting these steins, but also began collecting the other holiday steins for Oktoberfest and St. Patrick's Day. As a testament to the value of this collection, he recently auctioned off 270 of his steins for the total amount of $35,000.

He has no idea how large his collection is, but estimates that he easily has over 1,000 pieces. His collection ranges from modern collectibles like the Budweiser steins and Danbury Mint trucks to older, antique-type items.

Gum Ball Machine
$50

Anheuser-Busch
Beer Keg Bank
Value: N/E

Instead of using business cards, Adolphus Busch, co-founder of the Anheuser-Busch Company, used to give pocketknives to his better customers. Crumpley has a sample of one such pocketknife, valued at over $300. He also collects bottles and cans of every Anheuser-Busch product ever produced. Other Anheuser-Busch pieces in his collection include glassware, tap handles, signs of all shapes and sizes, Olympic pins, old magazine advertisements, trays and coasters.

Collecting Budweiser Items

Collecting the promotional, collectible and giftware items of a particular brewery is an innovative way of maintaining a breweriana collection. Not only does such a varied collection make it interesting to look at, it is also easy to display throughout your home, and the range of items can prove to be quite valuable on the secondary market.

Red Truck And
Airplane
Value: $110

Miniature Bud Cans
Value: $75/Set

Bulova Quartz Watch
Value: $120

Eagle Money Clip
w/Watch And Knife
Value: $80

Zippo Lighters
Value: $140/Set

Cans

Bob Forsythe became a beer can collector in a most unusual manner. In the 1980s, Forsythe was stationed in Iceland with the Air Force. He brought six empty beer cans along with him to help start

conversations with strangers in a new place. The beer cans sparked not only conversations, but also helped build Forsythe's collection. His friends who were stationed with him wrote home to request additional beer cans to expand the collection.

Bob Forsythe's cans are a record of his travels – and those of his friends, who have helped him build his collection.

Forsythe says that a person could spend a lot of money collecting beer cans, but he chooses not to. Still, his collection of nearly 6,000 beer cans is highly impressive. Forsythe has cans from Czechoslovakia and Yugoslavia. He also has various cans that he has collected in his travels to Europe and some that commemorate important moments in U.S. history.

Now that he is several years into his hobby, he has learned that cans that are unopened look better – therefore he pokes a hole at the bottom of each can and drains the beer out so that the can still looks new.

Forsythe says a good way to add to a collection is by what he calls "dumping" – rummaging through other people's trash or through dumpsters. As the saying goes, "One person's trash is another person's treasure."

Canadian Ace Ale
Canadian Ace Brewing Co.
Chicago, IL
Value: $100

Collecting Cans

Beer cans are an interesting item of breweriana because there are so many different kinds of cans to collect. You could collect by brewery, brand or different types of cans. Cone-shaped cans are the earliest kind of can, followed by those with pull-top lids and then push-back lids. Cans pose challenging storage issues, as they might rust under humid conditions (and with beer still in them), and they can be dented easily if they are mishandled.

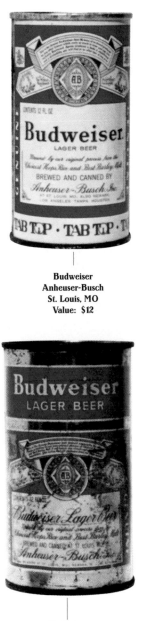

Budweiser
Anheuser-Busch
St. Louis, MO
Value: $12

Du Bois Export
Du Bois Brewing Co.
Du Bois, PA
Value: $120

Berghoff
Fort Wayne
Brewing Co.
Fort Wayne, IN
Value: $85

E & B Light Lager
Ekhart & Becker
Brewing Co.
Detroit, MI
Value: $150

Duquesne
Duquesne Brewing Co.
Stone Township, PA
Value: $150

Budweiser
Anheuser-Busch
St. Louis, MO
Value: $40

Menominee Champion
Menominee-Marinette
Brewing Co.
Menominee, MI
Value: N/E

Koller's Topaz
Koller Brewing Co.
Chicago, IL
Value: N/E

Frankenmuth
Air Free
Frankenmuth Brewing Co.
Frankenmuth, MI
Value: $120

Grain Belt
Minneapolis Brewing Co.
Minneapolis, MN
Value: $100

Hamm's
Theo Hamm Brewing Co.
St. Paul, MN
Value: $10

Gluek's
Gluek's Brewing Co.
Minneapolis, MN
Value: $125

Zhujiang Beer
Guangzhou, China
Value: N/E

Taiwan Beer
Taiwan
Value: N/E

Hatuey
Mexico
Value: N/E

Pabst Blue Ribbon Export
Pabst Brewing Co.
Peoria Heights, IL
Value: $50

Tuborg
Christmas Brew
Tuborg International
Copenhagen, Denmark
Value: N/E

Richbrau
Home Brewing Co.
Richmond, VA
Value: $140

Pfeiffer's
Pfeiffer Brewing Co.
Detroit, MI
Value: $25

Selecta
San Miguel Brewing Group
Manila, Philippines
Value: N/E

Pabst Blue Ribbon
Pabst Brewing Co.
Peoria Heights, IL
Value: $30

Coasters

George Barone's interest in breweriana started in college when he began collecting beer cans. Due to limited space in his college dorm room, he switched to collecting coasters, which were more readily available and took up less space. Presently, Barone estimates the size of his collection to number approximately 10,000 coasters.

George Barone has the right to be a boaster about his coasters – he has about 10,000 of them!

Barone collects strictly American coasters. He has coasters from different breweries representing many different regions of the country. The recent explosion in the popularity of microbreweries and brewpubs enables Barone to add to his collection extensively. He finds that many coasters are available for free from restaurants, brewpubs and microbreweries.

Barone has designed a web page for his collection, entitled Coaster Mania, which he maintains weekly. The site is located at *http://members.aol.com/gbarone/index.html* and is a great way for him to communicate with other collectors. It also provides a venue for people to trade and buy coasters from all over the world.

Yuengling's
D. G. Yuengling & Son
Pottsville, PA
Value: N/E

Coaster collecting is a relatively affordable hobby to get into. Coasters range in value anywhere from 20¢ to roughly $300. The majority of coasters, however, are available for an affordable $6 to $20.

Collecting Coasters

Tegestology is a word you might not be able to find in your Webster's Dictionary, but it is the official term for the act of collecting coasters. Coasters are a terrific item for someone new to breweriana to start collecting, because they are easy to find and easy to store. If you pick them up at a restaurant, brewpub or bar, they can also serve as great momentos of your travels and fun times with friends.

Budweiser
Anheuser-Busch
St. Louis, MO
Value: $25

Brewers' Best
Flock Brewing Co.
Williamsport, PA
Value: $65/each

E. Robinson's Sons Pilsener
E. Robinson's Sons
Scranton, PA
Value: $150

Narragansett
(illustrated by Dr. Seuss)
Narragansett
Brewing Co.
Cranston, RI
Value: $45

Anheuser-Busch
Anheuser-Busch
St. Louis, MO
Value: N/E

Coors
Coors Brewing Co.
Golden, CO
Value: N/E

Krueger's Beer & Ales
G. Krueger Brewing Co.
Newark, NJ
Value: $90

Krueger's Beer & Ales
G. Krueger Brewing Co.
Newark, NJ
Value: $60

Meister Bräu
Peter Hand Brewing
Co.
Chicago, IL
Value: $105

Gretz Beer
William Gretz Brewing Co.
Philadelphia, PA
Value: $85

Hungaria
The Bridgeport
Brewing Co.
Bridgeport, CT
Value: $90

Hyde Park
Hyde Park Brewing
Hyde Park, NY
Value: $35

John Eichler Brewing Co.
New York, NY
Value: $75

Goebel Beer
Goebel Brewing Co.
Detroit, MI
Value: $50

Old Nut Brown Ale
Duquesne Brewing Co.
Pittsburgh, PA
Value: $75

Red Fox Ale & Lager
Largay Brewing Co.
Waterbury, CT
Value: $30

Red Top Beer
Red Top Brewing Co.
Cincinnati, OH
Value: $160

Union Club Beer
Star Union Products Co.
Peru, IL
Value: $120

Old India Pale Ale
Commercial Brewing Co.
Boston, MA
Value: N/E

R & H Beer
Rubsam & Horrmann
Brewing Co.
Staten Island, NY
Value: $40

City Club Beer
Jacob Schmidt Brewing Co.
St. Paul, MN
Value: $45

Figurines

Collecting breweriana is a team effort for Ron and Sue Widdows of Peoria, Illinois. The driving force behind their collection is to preserve the history of the brewing and distilling industries. It's a highly personal quest for Sue as her great-great-uncle owned the well-known Kellerstrass distilleries in Kansas City and St. Louis.

Although the Widdows like to collect many kinds of breweriana figurines, the large portion of their collection falls into the category of "back bar" items. These are advertising items that are typically positioned on or behind a bar. They include such things as clocks, signs, mirrors, foam scrapers, plates and small figurines. These figurines are made from various materials, including metal, wood, plastic and plaster. The diversity of this breweriana category truly provides something for everyone.

Unlike some of today's collectors who conduct the majority of their shopping on the Internet, the Widdows enjoy visiting antique stores, flea markets and other hot spots for bargain hunters.

Blatz Brewery
Milwaukee, WI
Value: $45

The Widdows offer three suggestions for all collectors. First, a serious collector should join (if available) an organization for collectors in their area of interest. Second, collectors should read up on their area of interest, as this will help in bargain hunting. Third, collectors should try to buy the best piece available in their price range, instead of buying several less-expensive pieces.

Drewrys Beer
Drewrys Brewery
South Bend, IN
Value: $35

Collecting Beer Figurines

Beer figurines, or back bar items, as they are known in breweriana terminology, are terrific conversation starters. As innovative, eye-catching pieces, their original purpose was to be displayed in bars and advertise the beers sold there. Now they just look great as part of a personal breweriana collection.

Heineken Lager
Heineken N.V.
Amsterdam,
Netherlands
Value: $20

Rolling Rock
Latrobe Brewing Co.
Latrobe, PA
Value: $40

Miller High Life
Miller Brewing Co.
Milwaukee, WI
Value: $145/Set

Labatt's
Labatt Brewing Co.
London, Ontario
Value: $20

Pabst Blue Ribbon
Pabst Brewing Co.
Peoria Heights, IL
Value: $95

Rolling Rock
Latrobe Brewing Co.
Latrobe, PA
Value: $35

Labels

Seven years ago, Mike Hayes of Oakfield, Wisconsin, was intrigued by a colorful label on a bottle of the Mexican beer, Simpatico. His fascination compelled him to bring the label home to display and thus began his collection. Presently, Hayes has over 7,000 labels.

Labels can be collected either on or off the bottles. The best way for collecting labels is to purchase them separately, since soaking a label off a bottle can ruin the label's quality. A common method to display labels off of the bottle is to create a scrapbook.

Mike Hayes' goal is to collect a label from every beer made – and he's on his way, as he has over 7,000 of them!

Hayes, however, prefers labels to be displayed on the bottle, and about 4,800 of his labels are displayed as such. He often buys labels and bottles separately, and then glues the labels onto the bottles. He does extensive research into the kind of bottle originally used with the label and tries to match label and bottle up accordingly.

Tommy Bahama
Bungalow Brew
Paradise Brewing Co.
Sarasota, FL

Hayes' personal quest is to collect one label of every beer produced in the world. Finding labels is not a difficult task, as they are readily available for purchase on the Internet for a reasonable sum, and in some cases they can be acquired for free. Other places to look for labels include auctions, breweriana shows, antique malls, garage sales and liquor stores. Hayes suggests that new collectors join a breweriana organization, such as the American Breweriana Association, which can help collectors in get in touch with other like-minded collectors.

ABC Extra Pale Dry Beer
Maier Brewing Co.
Los Angeles, CA

Collecting Labels

Beer labels are easy to get and cost very little to purchase. The best way to start collecting labels is to write or call breweries and ask them to send you some. Most breweries will oblige without any problem, and might even send them to you for free, as long as you send them a self-addressed and stamped envelope for them to send you the labels in. If they do charge you, the charge will probably be quite minimal.

Alps Brau
Peter Hand Brewing Co.
Chicago, IL

Brooklyn Brewery
Brooklyn, NY

American Beer
American Brewery
Cumberland, MD

Black Horse Ale
Black Horse Brewery
Lawrence, MA

Bull Ice
Stroh Brewing Co.
Detroit, MI

Bud Light
Anheuser-Busch
St. Louis, MO

Carrabassett Pale Ale
Sugarloaf Brewing Co.
Carrabassett Valley, ME

McGuire's Irish Ale
McGuire's Brewing Co.
Pensacola, FL

Dominion Ale
Old Dominion Brewing Co.
Ashburn, VA

Cerveza Caliente
Minnesota Brewing Co.
St. Paul, MN

O'Brien's Harvest Ales
Hale's Ales
Seattle, WA

Frio Lager Beer
Frio Brewing Co.
San Antonio, TX

Honey B's Brown Ale
Mr. B's Brewing Co.
Pontiac, MI

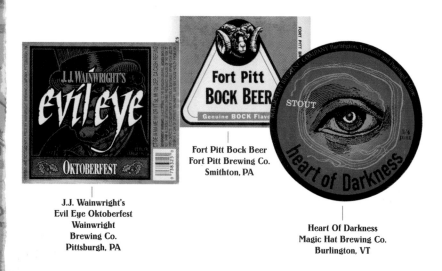

Fort Pitt Bock Beer
Fort Pitt Brewing Co.
Smithton, PA

J.J. Wainwright's
Evil Eye Oktoberfest
Wainwright
Brewing Co.
Pittsburgh, PA

Heart Of Darkness
Magic Hat Brewing Co.
Burlington, VT

12 FL.OZ.
(355 ML)

Anheuser-Busch.
Natural Light

Naturally Brewed Quality in a Light Beer

Natural Light
Anheuser-Busch
St. Louis, MO

Miller High Life
Miller Brewing
Company
Milwaukee, WI

Old Detroit Red Lager
Old Detroit
Brewing Co.
Frankenmuth, MI

Old German
Style Beer
Renner Company
Fort Wayne, IN

Oliver Ironman Pale Ale
Oliver Breweries Ltd.
Cambridge, MD

Oregon Hefeweizen
Oregon Ale & Beer Co.
Portland, OR

Pete's Wicked
Honey Wheat
Pete's Brewing Co.
Eden, NC

Red Tail Ale
Mendocino Brewing Co.
Hopland, CA

Pyramid Apricot Ale
Pyramid Breweries
Seattle, WA

Regional Beer Memorabilia – Boston

Dan Morean has items from many Boston-area breweries that no longer exist.

Dan Morean has been collecting breweriana for more than 20 years. He started collecting because a friend of his dragged him on collecting expeditions. It wasn't until he had been helping his friend for a few weeks that Morean became interested himself. A Tech Beer can from the Pittsburgh Brewing Company is what caught his eye and from then on, Morean was hooked.

Morean put his collecting on hold while he was in college and then later in law school. But several years after graduating from law school, Morean's interest was revived as he discovered some unique cans at an antique shop in Boston. Soon Morean began attending trade shows, where he was exposed to other breweriana items and he began collecting coasters, openers and old photographs of breweries in addition to cans. Since he worked in the Boston area, Morean added various items from the different breweries to his collection.

Boston Light Ale
Cone Top Can
1950
Boston Beer Co.
Value: $3,800

P.B. Ale
Pin
1910
Value: $250

Three years ago, Morean decided to leave the legal profession and devote his time to breweriana collecting. He constructed a web page, *www.breweriana.com*, which offers information for collectors and is also a site for trading, buying and selling. At any given time there are more than 2,000 items available at his site. In the future, Morean plans on expanding his collection to include breweriana pieces from Cleveland, Ohio.

Circa dates for this personal collection supplied by Dan Morean.

Collecting Regional Beer Memorabilia

A great way to focus your collecting hobby is to narrow it down to a specific region. One way to begin your collection is to research your local brewing history, which may feature many unique and long-forgotten brews. This collection features Boston-area breweriana, including bottles, cans and more. Just as Boston has played a significant role in the history of the United States, it has also played an important role in American brewing history.

A.G. Van Nostrand/
Bunker Hill Breweries
Tray
1905-1915
Value: $900

P.B. Bulldog
Pin
1900-1910
Value: $95

Pickwick Ale Light
Cone Top Can
1950
Haffenreffer
Value: $240

Fenway Lager
Bottle
1917
Fenway Breweries
Value: $50

Old Boston Brewery
Lithograph
1870s
Value: $6,000

Gamecock Ale
Flat Top Can
1950
Croft
Value: $2,400

Regional Beer Memorabilia – Philadelphia

A look at just one part of Don Fink's extensive breweriana collection.

Don Fink has always been a collector – even as a child when he collected Hot Wheels. As an adult, he has turned his love of collecting into a career, as he now owns and manages an auction house in Lansdale, Pennsylvania.

Fink started collecting beer cans at the age of 12. His interest started when some of his older friends told him they were going to construct a couch out of beer cans. Fink was excluded, so he decided to create his own beer can couch. However, once he had collected the cans, he was more interested in the artwork on the cans than in the couch. His collecting days began at that point.

Fink's Coaster
Early 1930s
Value: $70

In two years' time, Fink had amassed an amazing 2,500 beer cans. He became a member of the Beer Can Collecting Club of America and drove with his father to his first beer convention in Denver, Colorado.

Fink's Beer Bottles
Pre-Prohibition
Value: $15 each

Fink has since sold off part of that original collection and now limits his collection to breweriana from the town of Philadelphia and the Fink Brewery (no relation) in Harrisburg, Pennsylvania. He believes that the collection he has today is large enough to "fill a museum."

Circa dates for this personal collection supplied by Don Fink.

Collecting Regional Beer Memorabilia II

When deciding to collect by region, keep in mind that you don't have to stick to your own local area. Even beyond the big-time brewing meccas of St. Louis and Milwaukee, there are numerous areas of the country (and the world) that have a rich and wonderful brewing lore. This collection features tap handles, cans, signs and more from the Philadelphia area.

Esslinger's Beer Cans

Values:
#1. $1,000
#2. $450
#3. $350
#4. $300
#5. $500

Anton Stroebele
Lager Beer Sign
1880s
Value: $3,000

Esslinger's Beer
Sign
1930s
Value: $550

Erlanger Pony Deluxe
Coaster
1940s
Value: $20

Fink's Girl and Horse
Tray
1905
Value: $1,200

Esslinger's
Foam Scraper Holders
Pre-Prohibition
Value: $500

Black Eagle
Tap Marker
1930s
Value: $140

Fink's
Sign
1905
Value: $550

Golden Eagle Brewery
Stein
1890s
Value: $325

Gretz Beer
Tap Marker
1930s
Value: $135

Hohenadel
Tin Lithograph Sign
1930s
Value: $625

Indian Queen
Tap Handle
1930s
Value: $150

Hohen-Adel Bier
Coaster
Pre-Prohibition
Value: $70

Peerless Hercules Brau
Tray
1890s
Value: $650

Louis Bergoole
Steins & Bottles
Values:
#1. $20
#2. $1,100
#3. $550
#4. $20

Poth's Beer
Light-Up Sign
1930s
Value: N/E

**Premier Beer
Tray
1910s
Value: $350**

**Rex Beer
Tap Handle
1930s
Value: $160**

**Robert Smith Ale
Ashtray
Pre-Prohibition
Value: $100**

**Robert Smith Ale
Sign
1880s
Value: $3,500**

**Schmidt's Ale
Tin Sign
1930s
Value: $100**

**Schmidt's Ale
Tin Sign
1930s
Value: $100**

**Tannhaeuser
Glass Sign
1890s
Value: $3,000**

**Weisbrod & Hess
Tap Handle
1930s
Value: $140**

**Weger Bros.
Stein
Pre-Prohibition
Value: $175**

Steins

A retired electrician in Summerfield, Florida, Francis Slater has been collecting beer steins since 1976. He bought his first stein while on vacation in Belfast, Maine. The ceramic mug caught his eye because of the green porcelain frog attached to the inside bottom of the mug. "After that," Slater says, "things kind of got away from me."

Francis Slater loves his Budweiser steins.

Today Slater's collection has more than 200 steins and glasses in it and is valued between $5,000-$6,000. His collection primarily consists of Budweiser steins. He favors his complete collection of the St. Patrick's Day series (10 in all) and the Budweiser Oktoberfest series (four in all) which includes steins produced from 1991-1996. For each new stein Slater purchases, he drinks his favorite beer, Budweiser, from it before he places the stein on display.

For those collectors interested in collecting steins, Slater advises starting with one series that interests them, and collecting as many steins as possible for it. There are several different series, with varied themes, such as sports, wildlife, Christmas and winter scenes, so the spectrum is wide enough to fit any interest. Prices for new steins range between $20 to $30 and the more expensive limited edition steins are available for around $150 and up. All Budweiser steins come in a box with a certificate of authenticity. If you plan on selling your steins you may want to save the certificate and the original packaging. However, if you collect beer steins purely for enjoyment like Slater does, you may not have room to save 200 boxes!

"Covered Bridge"
Budweiser
Issued: 1984
Value: $20

Collecting Steins

Beer steins are great for drinking – but they also can be great for collecting! Steins became commonplace in 15th-century Europe during the time of the bubonic plague, which was believed to have been spread by flies. The hinged lids on beer steins were designed to keep the flies away, yet still allow the beer drinker to use one hand. Steins – both new and old – often feature elegant and unique designs and some can truly be considered works of art!

"Cameo Wheatland"
Budweiser
Issued: 1983
Value: $33

"An American Tradition"
Budweiser
Issued: 1990
Value: $25

"Bottled Treasure"
Budweiser
Issued: 1993
Value: N/E

"Chasing The Checkered Flag"
Budweiser
Issued: 1991
Value: $20

"Clydesdales"
Budweiser
Issued: 1976
Value: $170

"Erin Go Bud"
Budweiser
Issued: 1991
Value: $50

"Cobblestone Passage"
Budweiser
Issued: 1988
Value: $20

"Gridiron Legacy"
Budweiser
Issued: 1991
Value: $20

"Hometown Holiday"
Budweiser
Issued: 1994
Value: $20

"Horsehead"
Budweiser
Issued: 1987
Value: $45

"Lighting the
Way Home"
Budweiser
Issued: 1995
Value: $17

"Luck O' The Irish"
Budweiser
Issued: 1994
Value: $22

"Bud Man"
Budweiser
Issued: 1989
Value: $100

Mini Stein
Budweiser
Issued: 1992
Value: N/E

"Oktoberfest"
Budweiser
Issued: 1991
Value: $30

"Budweiser
Oktoberfest"
Budweiser
Issued: 1992
Value: $30

"1993 Budweiser
Oktoberfest"
Budweiser
Issued: 1993
Value: $25

"A Perfect Christmas"
Budweiser
Issued: 1992
Value: $22

"Par For The Course"
Budweiser
Issued: 1992
Value: $20

"Pot of Gold"
Budweiser
Issued: 1992
Value: $18

"The Season's Best"
Budweiser
Issued: 1991
Value: $23

"Special Delivery"
Budweiser
Issued: 1993
Value: $22

"Traditional Houses"
Budweiser
Issued: 1986
Value: $30

"Winter Evening"
Budweiser
Issued: 1989
Value: $24

"Tip O' The Hat"
Budweiser
Issued: 1995
Value: $16

Tap Handles

For Chris Cambareri of Cromwell, Connecticut, collecting breweriana runs in the family. More than 25 years ago, his father Joseph Cambareri and a partner, Jay Polke, opened a liquor store. They also began collecting beer cans, which Chris Cambareri now displays in the store. The breweriana bug first bit Cambareri about eight or ten years ago when the growth of microbreweries sparked his interest in tap handles.

Chris Cambareri sits in front of a beer display.

Cambareri began attaching them to the doors of the store's refrigerated section. From that moment on, as each beer representative came to the store, a tap handle was added to a cooler door. Soon all 12 cooler doors sported these new handles and there were still more brands vying for a spot. Today, Cambareri has about 200 handles, 72 of which he displays in his store and rest of which he keeps in boxes. Some of Cambareri's favorite handles are those from breweries that are no longer in existence. Cambareri actively adds to his collection by trading handles with customers and friends.

Bass Ale
Burton-on-Trent,
England
Value: $65

Traditionally, tap handles are used to dispense draft beer. They also advertise and inform customers of the different beer brands available in a bar. Tap handles range in price depending on the material of their construction. Newer, clear-acrylic tap handles can be purchased for around $5, whereas wooden hand-painted tap handles can range from $10 to $50 and porcelain tap handles can sell for over $100.

Budweiser
Door Knocker
Anheuser-Busch
St. Louis, MO
Value: N/E

Tap Handles

Tap handles are the beer drinker's equivalent to an ATM machine – they're used for frequent withdrawals (and at all hours of the day or night). But tap handles certainly have much more personality than the modern-day money-dispensing machines. They've been produced in all shapes and sizes, and can add the perfect decorative touch to your home bar.

Hammer & Nail
Brewers
Watertown, CT
Value: $140

Budweiser
Anheuser-Busch
St. Louis, MO
Value: N/E

Devil Mountain
Five Malt Ale
Devil Mountain Brewing
Cincinnati, OH
Value: N/E

Chester's Hard
Apple Cider
Kruger's Old
Maine Farm
North Stonington, CT
Value: N/E

Fuller's ESB
Fuller, Smith & Turner
Chiswick, England
Value: $40

Coors Light
Coors Brewing Company
Golden, CO
Value: N/E

Harpoon Dark
Harpoon Brewery
Boston, MA
Value: $60

Molson Golden
Molson Brewing Co.
Montreal, Canada
Value: $35

Ipswich Ale
Mercury Brewing Co.
Ipswich, MA
Value: $30

Magic Hat #9
Magic Hat
Brewing Company
South Burlington, VT
Value: N/E

Heineken
Heineken N.V.
Amsterdam,
Netherlands
Value: $75

Miller Lite
Miller Brewing
Company
Milwaukee, WI
Value: $25

Mystic Seaport
Pale Ale
The Shipyard
Brewing Co.
Portland, ME
Value: N/E

Miller Reserve
Velvet Stout
Miller Brewing
Company
Milwaukee, WI
Value: $40

Murphy's Irish Stout
Murphy Brewery
Cork, Ireland
Value: $60

Moosehead Beer
Moosehead Breweries
Limited
St. John, Canada
Value: $30

Samuel Adams
Summer Ale
The Boston
Beer Company
Boston, MA
Value: $50

Otter Creek Copper Ale
Otter Creek Brewing
Middlebury, VT
Value: N/E

Pete's Wicked Ale
Pete's Brewing Company
Eden, NC
Value: $35

Wild Irish Rogue
Rogue Ales
Newport, OR
Value: N/E

Samuel Adams
Cranberry Lambic
The Boston
Beer Company
Boston, MA
Value: $45

Atlantic Amber
New England
Brewing Co.
South Norwalk, CT
Value: N/E

Samuel Adams
Octoberfest
The Boston
Beer Company
Boston, MA
Value: $35

Old Gollywobbler
Brown Ale
Sea Dog
Brewing Company
Bangor &
Camden, ME
Value: N/E

Shipyard Export Ale
The Shipyard
Brewing Co.
Portland, ME
Value: $28

Trays

To Mark Rogers' friends and breweriana pals he is known as the "Trayman." This nickname is no exaggeration. Rogers' collection,

by his conservative estimate, includes more than 900 beer trays from North America that he has been collecting since the early 1970s. He has organized his collection into three different categories based on the name of the brewery, the location of the brewery or the theme depicted on the tray. He has beer trays ranging in value from $7 all the way up to $2,500.

Mark Rogers is sometimes known as the "Trayman."

In college, Rogers experimented with collecting all different types of breweriana, including bottles and signs. He finally settled on beer trays, partly because of their size and surface area. The larger surface of a beer tray provides more room for artwork and provides a more interesting visual experience for a collector.

Coors Brewing
Company
Golden, CO
13" x 10.5"
Value: $275

Rogers finds many of his beer trays on web sites like *eBay.com* but also acquires them at antique stores, flea markets, garage sales, auctions and special shows just for beer collectors. He has been with the hobby long enough that he has developed friendships with people throughout the country who scout out items on his wish list.

The American
Brewing Co.
St. Louis, MO
12"
Value: $750

Rogers feels that this is a fairly affordable hobby to get into. There are many good trays for beginners priced in the $8 to $20 range.

Trays

Beer trays date back to the late 1800s, when they were often the only form of advertisement that brewers had. While older beer trays were almost exclusively made out of tin, today's trays are usually produced out of plastic. Trays can be found in numerous shapes and sizes, but most are circular or oval and have a diameter ranging from 12 to 16 inches. A significantly smaller tray is most likely a "tip tray" used for providing change to bar customers.

Anheuser-Busch
Anheuser-Busch
St. Louis, MO
12"
Value: $750

Budweiser
Anheuser-Busch
St. Louis, MO
13"
Value: $140

Cream City
Brewing Co.
Milwaukee, WI
14"
Value: $330

Pioneer
Bridgeport Brewing
Company
Bridgeport, CT
12"
Value: $275

Brucks
Bruck Brewing
Cincinnati, OH
13.5" x 10"
Value: $60

Cruz Blanca
Cerveceria Cruz Blanca
Mexico
13"
Value: $140

Cruz Blanca
Cerveceria Cruz
Blanca
Mexico
12"
Value: $200

Bluebonnet Beer
Dallas Fort Worth
Brewing Co.
Texas
17.25" x 12"
Value: $140

Dixie Beer
Dixie Brewing Co.
New Orleans, LA
13"
Value: $90

Fox Lake Beer
Fox Lake Brewing Co.
Fox Lake, WI
13" x 10.5"
Value: $395

Jax
Jackson Brewing Co.
New Orleans, LA
13" x 10.5"
Value: $95

Primo Beer
Honolulu Brewing &
Malting Co.
Honolulu, HI
13"
Value: $2,600

John Gund
Brewing Co.
La Crosse, WI
12"
Value: $500

Lebanon Valley Beer
Lebanon Valley, PA
14"
Value: $125

Miller High Life
Miller Brewing
Company
Milwaukee, WI
13"
Value: $250

Menk's
Lexington St. Brewery
Louisville, KY
13.5" x 16.5"
Value: $1,300

Pacific Beer
Pacific Brewing And
Malting Co.
Tacoma, WA
12"
Value: $700

Tacoma Beer
Pacific Brewing Co.
San Francisco, CA
13"
Value: $800

Peoples Beer
Peoples Brewing Co.
Osh Kosh, WI
12"
Value: $65

Regal Beer
American Brewing Co.
Miami, FL
13"
Value: $50

Texas Pride
San Antonio Brewing Co.
San Antonio, TX
13.5" x 10.5"
Value: $300

Rainier
Seattle Brewing &
Malting Co.
Seattle, WA
13"
Value: $85

Golden Dawn
Sunrise Brewing Co.
Cleveland, OH
12"
Value: $300

Great Beer Recipes

Beer has been used in recipes since ancient times, and cooking with beer can be fun, easy, healthy and above all, tasty. Chef Robert Mattia-Slater is the head chef of a popular Connecticut restaurant, and he has shared some of his best beer recipes here.

Chef Robert Mattia-Slater reveals some of his favorite beer recipes.

Authentic Early American Beer Barrel Bread

Ingredients

3 cups self-rising enriched flour

2 tablespoons sugar

12 oz. ale

Directions

• Preheat oven to 375°F.

• Evenly grease a loaf pan.

• Combine flour and sugar in a large mixing bowl.

• Pour in bottle of beer and stir ingredients together. Keep stirring until it forms a dough.

This tasty bread goes great with any meal.

• Pour into greased loaf pan.

• Bake for 1 hour.

Robert's Spicy Cheddar & Ale Soup

Ingredients

1 lb. carrots

1 medium-sized onion

1/2 lb. butter

2 cups chicken bouillon

2 teaspoons ground dry mustard (do not substitute other mustards)

1/4 teaspoon white pepper

1 cup flour

12 oz. ale

Robert's Spicy Cheddar and Ale Soup is the perfect appetizer for when guests come to visit.

1 teaspoon hot sauce or cayenne pepper (optional)

2 quarts half & half

1 teaspoon kosher salt

1-1/2 lbs. extra-sharp cheddar, shredded

Directions

• Shred carrots and finely dice onion.

• In medium-sized soup pot over medium-high heat, melt butter and add shredded carrots and onion. Sauté for 10 minutes or until the vegetables are wilted and almost cooked.

• Add ground dry mustard, white pepper and flour to the vegetables to make a roux. Keep scraping bottom of pan to keep from burning. Cook on medium-low heat, stirring constantly for 5 minutes.

• Add chicken bouillon and stir thoroughly to avoid lumps.

• Add beer to roux, stirring constantly. Let sit on medium-low heat for 5 minutes (it might smell like it's burning, but it is not). Do not let the mixture boil.

• Add hot sauce or cayenne pepper (if using), half & half and kosher salt and bring it almost to a boil.

• At 165°F, slowly add cheese, a little bit at a time. Let simmer on medium-low heat for 5 minutes.

Makes 16 8-oz. servings.

Papa Fran's German-Style Red Cabbage

Ingredients

1 large head of red cabbage, sliced thin

2-3 Macintosh apples

1 small onion

24 oz. ale

1 teaspoon cinnamon

1 teaspoon nutmeg

1 stick butter

1 cup white granulated sugar

1 cup brown sugar

1 cup cider vinegar

This dish is sure to disappear from any dinner table quickly!

Directions

• Combine all ingredients in a large pot.

• Cook on medium heat for 4 hours, stirring occasionally.

Roast Pork with Roasted New Potatoes and Vegetables with Apple Beer Gravy

Ingredients

3 lbs. pork loin

1/2 teaspoon kosher salt

1/2 teaspoon coarse black pepper

2 tablespoons rosemary

3 lbs. new potatoes (halved)

1 lb. large carrots, jullienned

2 medium onions, sliced

3 cloves garlic, sliced

salt and pepper to taste

1-1/2 cups hard cider

1/2 cup water

1/4 cup flour

The apple beer gravy is the crowning glory of this roast pork.

Directions

- Pre-heat oven to 350ºF.

- Rub pork loin with salt, pepper and rosemary.

- Place pork loin in center of roasting pan and cover with lid. Place pan in middle rack of oven, and cook covered for 1 hour.

- Remove from oven. Pour off drippings and save them in a bowl.

- Add potatoes, carrots, onions and garlic around the pork loin in the roasting pan.

- Season with salt and pepper.

- Cover and return to oven for 45 minutes.

• Remove cover and pour hard cider over the roast and vegetables and return to oven uncovered for 20 minutes or until vegetables are cooked through. Remove from oven and drain liquid into saucepan, adding reserved drippings.

• Place saucepan on stove and heat drippings to a boil. While this boils, mix together flour and water (be sure to blend well so there are no lumps). Slowly add mixture to boiling stock, stirring until it thickens.

Chocolate Porter Cake and Frosting

Cake Ingredients

3/4 cup and 2 tablespoons salted butter

2-1/4 cups and 1/4 cup cake flour

2 teaspoons baking powder

1/2 teaspoon baking soda

1/2 teaspoon salt

Beer can play a part in every course of your special meal – even dessert!

3 eggs, separated, at room temperature

1-1/3 cups sugar

3 oz. unsweetened baker's chocolate, melted

1 cup porter or other dark beer, flat

Cake Directions

• Preheat the oven to 375°F.

• Lightly grease two 9-inch cake pans or one 9 x 13-inch cake pan with 2 tablespoons butter and dust with 1/4 cup of flour. Shake out and discard any excess flour and set the pans aside.

• Mix together the remaining flour with the baking powder, baking soda, and salt. Set aside.

• Beat the egg whites with 2 tablespoons of sugar until stiff peaks begin to form.

• With an electric mixer, cream together the remaining sugar with 3/4 cup butter until light in texture.

• One at a time, beat in the egg yolks.

• Stir in the melted chocolate and the beer.

• Gradually add flour mixture to the beer and chocolate mixture.

• With a rubber spatula, fold in the egg whites.

• Scrape the batter into the cake pan(s), and bake in the middle of the oven 30-35 minutes or until a toothpick inserted in the center comes out clean.

• Remove the pan(s) from the oven and let the cakes cool.

Chef Robert shows off his delicious creations.

Frosting Ingredients

1 lb. semi-sweet chocolate chips

2 tablespoons salted butter

5 tablespoons porter or other dark beer, flat

5 tablespoons milk

Frosting Directions

• Soften the chocolate chips and butter in a double boiler (the chips should be soft, but still hold their shape) and remove from heat.

• Using an electric beater, beat the chocolate and butter until smooth, about 1 minute.

• Beat in the porter and milk, one tablespoon at a time, until the mixture is soft and shiny.

• Remove the cakes from the pans before frosting the layers.

Beer Lingo

Whether you're a home-brewer, breweriana collector or just a fan of the suds, you should know your beer lingo.

alcohol by volume – alcohol content of beer, as a percentage of volume of alcohol per volume of beer

alcohol by weight – alcohol content of beer, as a percentage of weight of alcohol per weight of beer

ale – type of beer produced with top-fermenting yeast, fermented at a higher temperature than lagers

barley – cereal grain that is most often used in brewing

beer – a fermented beverage made from several different malted grains and usually seasoned with hops

bitter – English-style beer with a generous amount of hops (thus the name "bitter")

Sierra Nevada Pale Ale, Bass Ale and Pete's Wicked Ale are all ales.

bock – a dark, rich German beer

body – the "fullness," "weight" or "thickness" of beer on the tongue, ranging from thin- to full-bodied

breweriana – all manner of beer-related collectibles and memorabilia, such as coasters, mugs, cans, trays and the like

brewpub – establishment that brews and serves its own beer

conditioning – final fermentation process that occurs after beer has been placed in a container such as a cask or a bottle

dry-hopping – adding dry hops to increase bitterness and hoppy aroma of the beer

fermentation – the breakdown of sugar into carbon dioxide and alcohol by yeast

hard cider – an alcoholic beverage that is produced through the fermentation of apples

hops – a plant used to impart a bitter flavor to beer

India pale ale – British ale with strong, bitter flavor and generally light color

lager – type of beer produced with bottom-fermenting yeast, fermented at a lower temperature than ales; characterized by crisp, smooth flavor

malt – barley that has been steeped in water, sprouted and kilned

mouthfeel – how a beer "feels" on the tongue, be it in terms of temperature, carbonation, body, bitterness and the like

pasteurization – the heating of beer after fermentation in order to reduce the risk of contamination

porter – a dark ale thought to have been named for England's laborers (such as porters), its intended market

Reinheitsgebot – German purity law enacted in early 16th century requiring all German beer to be made only with yeast, hops, malted grains and water

stout – a thick, black ale that generally has has a rich head and a smoky flavor

wort – the sweet mashed barley and water mixture before the addition of yeast

yeast – single-celled members of the fungus family *Saccharomyces* that consume sugars and produce carbon dioxide and alcohol

Guinness, known for its thick head and dark color, is a popular stout.

Index

In this index you will find the page number of every beer, non-alcoholic brew, hard cider and hard lemonade mentioned in this guide. Pages are listed in alphabetical order, and bold numbers are the page of primary mention.

A Budweiser neon sign shows a lizard from a popular advertising campaign.

A Michelob coaster speaks for itself.

I.C. Light is packaged in black, silver and yellow.

A Molson Golden neon sign features the beer's
trademark maple leaf.

Samuel Adams beers are available
throughout the country.

Saranac fans can show their appreciation
for the beer through a variety of clothing.

Acknowledgements

CheckerBee Publishing would like to extend a very special thank you to John Stacey, Alan Newman, Paul Farthing, Tony and Joey at Elm City Brewing Company and the folks at Coach's in Hartford, Conn., and Player's Pub in Cromwell, Conn., who all contributed their valuable time to help us with this book. Photo credits: Corbis – pg. 114, Daybreak Imagery – pg. 52.